Shaping Organisational Culture
in Local Government

Managing Local Government Series

Human Resource Management in Local Government (second edition)
by Alan Fowler

Performance Management in Local Government (second edition)
by Steve Rogers

Renewing Public Management: an agenda for local governance
by Michael Clarke

Understanding the Management of Local Government: its special purposes, conditions and tasks (second edition) by John Stewart

Shaping Organisational Cultures in Local Government

Janet Newman

General Editors:
Michael Clarke and John Stewart

PITMAN PUBLISHING

in association with the
Institute of Local Government Studies

To Kieron Walsh, mentor and friend

PITMAN PUBLISHING
128 Long Acre, London WC2E 9AN

A Division of Pearson Professional Limited

First published in Great Britain 1996

© Pearson Professional Limited 1996

British Library Cataloguing in Publication Data
A CIP catalogue record for this book can be obtained from the British Library.

ISBN 0 273 61987 X

10 9 8 7 6 5 4 3 2 1

Typeset by Phoenix Photosetting, Chatham, Kent
Printed and bound in Great Britain by Redwood Books, Trowbridge, Wiltshire.

The Publishers' policy is to use paper manufactured from sustainable forests.

Contents

Editors' foreword

This book is one of a series of management handbooks published by Pitman Publishing in association with the Institute of Local Government Studies in the School of Public Policy at the University of Birmingham. The series is designed to help those concerned with management in local government to meet the challenge of the late 1990s. It is based on the belief that no period has been so important for local authorities to have effective management, responsive to both citizen and customer.

The mid 1990s have brought reorganisation to local authorities in Scotland, Wales and parts of England. No local authority, however, can escape the need to keep under continuous review its political and managerial structures and processes. All councils are caught up in far-reaching changes. Some of these come from local determination and decision, others from central government policy and yet others from deeper changes in society. New problems, issues and opportunities demand from local governments a capacity to respond in new ways. They have to become closer to their local communities, their public and the wide range of institutions and organisations involved in the governance of localities; they need to find imaginative solutions to the ever more complex problems of public policy; they have to manage their resources to achieve value for money and value in the services they provide; and they have to achieve effective management in all their activities. These are formidable challenges for the managers – and the politicians – involved.

There are plenty of management books, but this series is distinct. Its starting point is the need for emphasis on developing effective management in local government, associated with the need to take account of the particular nature of local government. The series sets out to be succinct and to be useful in the practical day-to-day world as well as being designed to be used as a prompt to management improvement.

In no sense are we pretending that this or other books in the series will show a *single way* to manage the local authority. Management is not like that. Our intention is to explore ideas and questions in order to help fashion the most helpful and effective approach to the local situation. We believe that local authority politicians and managers should draw on as wide a range of experience as possible but that this should be set in the context of the special purposes, conditions and tasks of local government. We hope that this book contributes to that end.

Professor Michael Clarke, Head of School of Public Policy
University of Birmingham

Professor John Stewart, Institute of Local Government Studies
in the School of Public Policy, University of Birmingham

Acknowledgements

I would like to thank the local authorities who gave their time and help as part of the 'Managing Change in Uncertain Times' project supported by the Local Government Management Board, and all of the local authorities and managers who have shared their experience and ideas with me in recent years.

Introduction

This book is about how local authorities can respond to the challenges of change by shaping and renewing organisational cultures. It is organised around four main themes.

The context of cultural change

Chapter 1, *The challenge of cultural change*, highlights the importance of organisational culture for local authorities seeking to respond to the challenges they face.

Cultural frameworks

This part of the book is intended to help managers and members begin to identify the kinds of changes that may be required in their own authority, department or team.

Chapter 2, *Understanding culture*, develops a framework for understanding the diversity and internal complexity of the cultures of local government.

Chapter 3, *Cultural analysis*, sets out methods for analysing the culture of a local authority, department or unit.

Chapter 4, *Mapping the culture*, provides tools for exploring the strengths and weaknesses of the different cultures within a local authority.

Cultural change

This part of the book is designed to help local authorities develop and shape the process of cultural change.

Chapter 5, *Cultural change: developing the approach*, identifies a range of approaches which can be matched to the purpose and requirements of an individual local authority.

Introduction

... *nd the vision: developing a programme of change*, explores
Chapte... local authorities seeking to bring about cultural change.
strate...

..., *Leading change*, identifies success factors for local government
Ch... whether chief executives or politicians, directors or team leaders, in
le... role in leading change and managing transition.
th...

...ter 8, *Developing a learning culture*, explores how a local authority can
de...lop its capacity to change and to learn from change.

Cultural renewal

The final chapters explore the cultural impact of the successive waves of change through the 1980s and into the 1990s, and set out emerging agendas for local authority politicians and managers.

Chapter 9, *Strategy, culture and change: a question of balance*, demonstrates how a local authority can identify and redress imbalance in its culture.

Chapter 10, *Cultural change and cultural renewal*, argues that new ways of thinking about culture and identity must be at the heart of local authority's search for new roles and purposes in the next decade and beyond.

The approach of the book

The book is intended to be both critical and practical. It aims to be of practical value to managers by providing tools to aid in the diagnosis of issues facing their authority, and techniques and approaches to draw on in the management of change. In doing so, however, the aim is to go beyond some of the rather simplistic recipes for 'managing culture' found in much of the literature. A broader appreciation of organisational culture and change means drawing on a range of concepts and ideas: for example those of cultural differentiation, cultural diversity, dynamic change, power and conflict, cultural capacity, and organisational balance. The book, then, attempts to link theory and practice in an integrated way.

While the structure of the chapters varies, some common components include:

■ a brief summary of chapter contents;

■ questions for readers to consider in applying the ideas to their own authority;

■ quotes highlighting the experience of local authority managers;

■ case studies drawn from a range of organisations and extracts from the literature on culture;

■ a review of the main ideas of the chapter.

1

The challenge of cultural change

THIS CHAPTER:

- Outlines a range of the challenges faced by local authorities.
- Explores the importance of cultural change in responding to the challenges.
- Highlights the importance of cultural renewal as well as cultural change.

Local authorities have in recent years faced a number of challenges which have led to radical reviews of their political and management arrangements. As well as having to respond to new climates of cost constraints and a raft of new legislation, local authorities have sought to:

- develop responsive, flexible and user-centred services;
- develop a wider 'governance' role;
- shape new patterns of working in partnership with other agencies;
- devolve and decentralise decision-making;
- become more concerned with quality;
- respond to diversity both externally and internally;
- prepare for the building of new local authorities as a result of local government review.

This chapter explores the importance of new political cultures and management styles, and of finding new direction and purpose for local government. Each of these depends on fundamental cultural changes: that is, changes to the beliefs, values, practices, ways of working and patterns of relationship within a local authority, and a transformation of its relationships with users, communities, and partners.

Flexible, responsive and user-centred services

The first set of challenges concerns local government as the deliverer of local services. The primacy of this role has historically underpinned the departmental organisation of both policy and management arrangements. This departmentalism has been buttressed by traditional committee structures and by the professional power bases of staff. Within departments, service delivery has traditionally been based on the principles of bureaucracy, hierarchy and functionalism, with a uniform service to all being delivered through tiers of control, and with work divided according to function (with, for example, different aspects of a housing problem of a single customer being dealt with by different functions within a housing department). Each of these principles is being fundamentally questioned as local authorities recognise the importance of flexibility, responsiveness and diversity in the way services are delivered. Hierarchical control is shifting as responsibility is devolved and organisational structures flattened. The organisation of the work itself is increasingly being planned around the requirements of customers and communities, rather than divided up into separate functions which the service user must navigate.

'One-stop shops', 'learning from service users' initiatives, and the devolution of responsibility to front line staff are all attempts to change the ways in which services are delivered. These do, however, often create tensions between the traditional departmental cultures and the emerging user-oriented cultures of local government, reflected in tensions within the member role as the role and power of service committees are challenged. More fundamentally the general shift towards a consumer culture potentially weakens the wider democratic and political culture of local government. Managing these tensions forms one of the key challenges faced by local government.

Developing the 'governance' role

These cultural changes in the ways in which services are delivered are not the whole picture. Many local authorities are attempting to develop roles and purposes which go beyond service delivery to encompass 'community governance'. This means, firstly, a concern for the problems and issues faced by local communities which transcend the traditional focus of departments and committees: for example issues of crime, public safety, poverty, health, the environment. These issues require multi-functional, multi-disciplinary and multi-agency activities which do not sit easily within bureaucratic and hierarchical organisational cultures, and are not easily accommodated within the established power bases of members. While restructuring departments into divisional groupings can facilitate a focus on key corporate agendas, it does not always do so. Nor is creating a common culture within new divisions an easy matter.

The second element of the 'governance' model is concerned with an expanded political concept of local government as empowering and enabling local communities. Many local authorities are now seeking to open up decision-making processes through decentralised management and the setting up of area committees with devolved powers. Some are also seeking to empower particular groups (tenants, disability groups, youth groups and so on) to take decisions on their own behalf. A few are seeking to stimulate public involvement in wider political processes through innovations in democratic practice.

These developments potentially turn local authority cultures 'upside down', requiring staff, managers and members to adopt new attitudes and orientations, to think and act in new ways, and to develop inclusive rather than distanced relationships with the public. Governance is concerned with the management of influence rather than the exercise of direct control. It depends on listening, facilitation, and collaboration skills rather than the provision of tailor made solutions to professionally defined problems. In John Stewart's terms, it requires working *for* the public and *with* the public, rather than simply providing services *to* the public (Stewart 1995).

Working through partnerships

The last decade has seen radical changes to the role of local government. Local authorities have had to respond to a reduction in their power to control their environment. They have had to develop an approach to bringing about change for the communities they serve through the exercise of influence and the development of partnerships. The growth of partnership arrangements presents a further challenge to traditional cultures based on hierarchy and control. Effective partnership working requires a signficant cultural shift within the local authority as a whole. External working needs to be supported by internal collaboration and networking. Basic assumptions may also need to change. Kerley argues that initiating and progressing change through a network of partnership arrangements will require a very different range of management and information systems to those in place within many councils, and will also require a change of attitude among councillors and council leaders:

> *Councils will have to adjust to the expectation that they can no longer instruct and expect obedience. ... The assumption that the council and its committees are at the centre of the known universe will come under increasing pressure* (Kerley 1994 p. 197).

Changing political and management relationships

Each of these challenges has had implications for political and management relationships and patterns of control. Power is becoming both more dispersed and more centralised. The requirement that local authorities take a longer term strategic view, rather than being led by short term budgetary processes and incremental policy adjustments, has led to some centralisation of power either to a core political group within the majority party, or to a central group of lead members and officers. Whatever the arrangement, there is a requirement for leadership, vision and direction in order to deal with the multiple challenges which local authorities face. This often means smaller management teams and more responsibility for leading members.

At the same time initiatives to decentralise power through neighbourhood officers, area committees, neighbourhood forums and so on require members to develop stronger local advocacy and representational roles. Partnership working requires members to engage in the management of influence to a much more extensive degree, and this requires new skills and a high level of both political and management support. The development of management by contract rather than by direct control of services also requires a shift in the political culture. Overall the role of members in setting strategic goals and monitoring and reviewing performance is growing in importance, while more and more control over the detail of implementation is being devolved to managers or is being exercised through the contracting process.

The relationship between committee roles, local roles and partnership activities, and between direct and indirect forms of political control over services, may be very unclear. What is clear, however, is the critical importance of the political culture – the values, assumptions and ways of working which members have developed over time, what members view as important, what is taught to new members, and so on – to the culture of the local authority as an organisation, and the perception of its value by the community as a whole.

4

Organisational and management changes

Many of these processes are mirrored internally within local authorities. Traditional forms of authority and control, based on regulation, supervision and instruction flowing down from the top of an organisation and reaching all who work within it, have become less effective. Flatter organisations, and working across boundaries with other agencies, place more emphasis on the need to manage horizontally rather than vertically. It is getting harder for the centre to control everything directly. There is more reliance on managing through influence and through attempting to generate shared goals and values.

This requires profound cultural changes. Building a new climate of commitment and ownership depends on an emphasis on communication, participation and employee involvement, together with good staff development, appraisal, and performance management systems. Many local authorities are making positive developments in these areas through seeking Investors in People accreditation and through a variety of Human Resources Management techniques. But more is needed, and many local authorities now talk in terms of 'empowering' staff. One reason for this lies in the growing importance of quality.

Culture as the foundation of quality

Most local authorities have been developing approaches to quality in recent years, and many have realised that it is not something which can be done at the margins or as an add-on to the rest of everyday practice. Some quality initiatives have been successful in terms of winning BS 5750 accreditation, but have not been seen as having delivered much from the customer's point of view. Many others have withered and some have died because quality has been treated as just one more corporate initiative, and because issues of cultural change have not been seriously addressed. For quality to be meaningful it requires the empowerment of employees nearest the customer, and this means a revolution in internal authority relationships, 'inverting' the traditional pyramid of control. Authority must be delegated to the lowest possible level, and the management role transformed into one of 'supporting' the front line and solving problems arising in the internal quality chain.

CULTURE AND QUALITY

An organisation with a culture oriented towards quality is one in which:

1 Innovation is highly valued.

2 Status is secondary to performance and contribution.

3 Leadership is a function of action, not position.

4 Rewards are shared through the work of teams.

5 Development, learning and training are seen as critical paths to sustainability.

6 Empowerment to achieve challenging goals supported by continued development and success provides a climate for self-motivation.

Source: Morgan and Murgatroyd, *Total Quality Management in the Public Sector,* 1994.

None of this can be achieved in the context of rigid or hierarchical cultures. Delivering quality in a user-centred way is not just about what happens at the point of service delivery. Many studies have shown that the way in which front line staff treat customers is directly related to the style with which their managers treat them. Change, then, is not just a matter of 'customer care' training or 'quality circles', but requires an organisation to address deeper cultural patterns which reproduce themselves over time.

The challenge of diversity

While most local authorities have traditionally seen themselves as pursuing 'equal opportunities', with more or less vigour, it is evident that new thinking is now required. A particular challenge for local authorities has been that of responding to the issues raised by groups who have traditionally been marginalised by the organisation, whether externally (users) or internally (staff). Rather than delivering a universal service to all in the same way, the ethos of responsiveness and flexibility requires local authorities to respond to a diversity of needs and requirements. Quality, then, means not just ensuring standardisation but must incorporate issues of diversity.

This has significant cultural implications. The ability of strong local authority cultures to reproduce themselves in their own image needs to be checked so that the perpetuation of old power bases is not automatic. Such changes are needed to ensure that women, black and ethnic minority groups and other marginalised voices within the community can be drawn into the shaping of the future. Diversity must be seen as a major strength in the renewal of local authority values and in the broadening of management approaches and styles. However this presents a major challenge for the ways in which 'organisational culture' has traditionally been understood, and cultural processes managed.

The challenge of local government review

Local Government Review has profound implications for both political and organisational cultures. It brings with it the break-up of existing cultures, and the loyalties, identifications and commitments on which they were based. It requires local authorities on which the new unitary authorities are to be based to attempt to rebuild their organisations, including new functions, new members, new staff, around a single common culture. Both processes of change will be difficult. Old loyalties may be transferred to the new authorities, creating a strongly fragmented culture riven by 'us' and 'them' divisions. Small local authorities based on a strong culture of openness and informality may find this hard to sustain when required to double their size. The local authorities who are to disappear face particular challenges in supporting staff through the process of cultural transition, and the 'new' local authorities need to respect the strengths of old allegiances as well as providing strong leadership around a future vision. The 'starting with a clean sheet of paper' approach to the creation of new authorities is likely to exacerbate the problems of cultural change.

The challenge of cultural renewal

The final, and perhaps most important, challenge is that of taking local authorities beyond the 'cultural impoverishment' which has often resulted from a decade or more of a primary focus on cost cutting, efficiency seeking and the predominant 'value for money' climate of the 1980s. The cultures of local government have traditionally been based around strong sets of values: public service values, civic values, the values of professionalism, probity and stewardship. These values were enshrined in the cultures of bureaucracy and paternalism which have been criticised in recent years.

However there are dangers that in developing more responsive, flexible and effective management cultures, the value base itself becomes unclear. Is 'efficiency' a concept which is likely to inspire and motivate staff? Is 'quality' a means of doing something or is it becoming an end in its own right? How can the demoralising effects of successive waves of cost cutting be redressed? How can values such as democracy, accountability and equity be sustained

7

alongside the requirement to become businesslike and to meet the challenges of competition and legislative change?

The importance of redefining culture in the process of setting purpose and direction is stressed by Ranson and Stewart:

> *The development of public management requires a shift in organisational culture to express the purposes and conditions of the public domain. If the challenge facing the public domain is to be met, public organisations need to create a capacity for cultural change: the central code of the culture is to* think public (Ranson and Stewart 1994 p. 245, [author's emphasis]).

Although there are difficulties around how 'the public' is to be defined, who has access to the 'public domain' and how issues of diversity are to be incorporated into 'thinking public', the role of local authorities in opening up and contributing to public discourse is an essential requirement for the process of cultural renewal in local government. I shall return to this theme in the final chapter.

An understanding of the cultures of the communities they serve can also help local authorities to respond to the complex social agendas and issues of the late twentieth century. It can support them in developing new ways of working with and through other agencies and organisations to develop coherent responses to new demands. Finally, and most importantly, the culture of a local authority – or of a specific department, service team or local office – has a very strong impact on how users and others view the authority. Reputation is based less on 'official' means of communication (publicity leaflets, brochures, annual reports) than on a host of myriad impressions based on how things 'feel' at the point of service delivery, at community events, in joint agency meetings and elsewhere. Together these forge a local authority reputation – and once forged, such reputations are very hard to change.

The importance of culture in meeting the challenges

Cultural change lies at the heart of responses to each of these challenges. It involves not just a change of departmental or divisional cultures, but of those of the corporate centre; not just a transformation of management cultures but of political cultures; and not just the cultures of a local authority as an organisation, but of its patterns of interaction with the wider 'public culture' of the communities and localities it serves.

Many local authorities have embarked on ambitious cultural change programmes in recent years. Cultural change has been seen as essential to the complex and difficult transformations which they wished to embrace – those of becoming more flexible and responsive, more user-centred, more quality focused, more 'businesslike' and so on. These all required not merely technical or systems changes, but a significant shift in values and attitudes: in how people thought about their jobs, in the ways in which 'success' was judged, and in the behaviour and interactions through which organisational practices are reproduced from day to day.

Peters and Waterman's *In Search of Excellence* (1982), on which many local authorities initially drew, depicted successful organisations as being those which were 'rich in culture' or which had a 'strong culture', sustained by a system of shared beliefs, values and habits. Pascale and Athos's *The Art of Japanese Management* (1981), Ouchi's *Theory Z* (1981) and other key texts all drew attention to the importance of guiding values in improving company performance. The development of 'corporate cultures' with a shared drive and common mission was etsablished as a key to organisational success (Deal and Kennedy 1982; Denison 1990). While the direct relationship between culture and performance suggested in some of these texts has since been criticised, a focus on culture remains a vital element in delivering responses to new demands and requirements.

Culture as a source of integration

More recently, issues of culture have become significant in the context of internal and external fragmentation. Recent cycles of change and restructuring have created new divisions: between purchasers and providers, clients and contractors, and between business units potentially in competition with each other for resources. These processes create some key dilemmas and tensions: for example:

– *How can local authorities attempt to develop a common organisational ethos as a response to structural fragmentation?*

Many local authorities are attempting to introduce greater devolution and/or decentralisation at the same time as they are seeking a stronger corporate response to issues of concern to the community as a whole.

– *How can local authorities minimise internal competition which may result from business cultures?*

The purchaser/provider framework brings a greater awareness of costs, and more responsive providers. But it can also produce some rigidities in contracts, roles and the specification of services. There can sometimes be a 'playing shop' mentality, or extreme posturing by those in both purchasing and providing roles. There may also be tensions and some discomfort in reconciling the commercial approach with a public sector ethos. One authority talked of an emerging concern to 'keep faith' with the public sector base and to modify the internal market philosophy.

– How can local authorities build relationships and collaborative processes which span purchaser–provider or client–contractor splits?

One of the issues which many local authorities introducing purchaser/ provider splits have been struggling with is how far the separation should go, and at what levels of the hierarchy integration should occur. Levels of formality around the internal and external contracting processes vary considerably, but it is evident that some form of collaboration is essential to deliver quality services to users.

Local authorities seeking to build flexible and responsive organisations have followed different routes. No one blueprint can be determined. But these questions illustrate the importance of developing capacity through both structures and culture, and of balancing the effects of each upon the other. A focus on culture seems to offer a means of developing shared goals and values in an era in which the unity of local authority purpose and practice has been increasingly hard to sustain. It also provides a means to ensure coherence between different or succesive change initiatives.

Culture and management approach

Cultural change offers an approach through which local authority purpose can be restated and major transformations put into place. But while there have been some remarkable successes, there have also been disappointments. We have come to realise that there is more to cultural change than the communication of a new vision, however enthusiastically this may be done. The production of a new 'mission' statement may appear shallow and hollow to front line staff struggling with diminishing resources and increasing demands. Corporate videos designed to promulgate the new message may produce cynicism rather than inspiration. New cultural goals and values may sound good but mean little in practice. Staff, managers and members may learn to speak the new language but carry on working in the old ways. We have learned that people cannot be viewed as the passive recipients of cultural change programmes: they actively shape their own meanings and interpret the world through the values which they bring from outside the organisation, as well as those which they learn within it.

As a result, we have begun to move away from the idea of cultural management as a 'quick fix' way of transforming organisations. But culture remains a centrally important idea in current thinking about people, management, organisations and change. Culture means recognising the importance of the informal and qualitative aspects of management, and draws attention to the implicit and even subversive dimensions of organisational life.

Anthony (1994) has argued that cultural change is a slow process, which can be assisted but not controlled. That is why this book is written in terms of shaping rather than managing culture. Shaping the process of change means attempting to balance different pressures and requirements, and dealing with the 'unintended consequences' of change. It also means not just delivering this particular change, but developing the *overall capacity* of the organisation as a whole through the way it is accomplished.

Building cultural capacity

The process of managing change has become more complex as local government has had to deal with multiple and interacting changes. Local authorities have struggled to respond to new agendas driven by central government, in which cycles of change have been overlaid on each other with little time for reflection or consolidation. Change has itself become more complex, with multiple changes interacting with each other across the work of an authority. Many of the changes we are concerned with today can be characterised as 'open ended' rather than 'closed'. Rather than change being a matter of moving from fixed point A to fixed point B, different change processes will interact with each other, leading towards an uncertain future.

All of this means that conventional sequential models of change, such as rational planning models of goals–plans–implementation–review, are sometimes less than effective. Lewin's 'Unfreezing–change–refreezing' model, often used in discussions of cultural change, is also flawed since it implies greater closure (the possibility of 'refreezing') than is possible or desirable in practice. Nadler and Tushman (1989) characterise major change processes in terms of a series of multiple transitions, incomplete transitions, and uncertain future states.

11

This new context means that as well as delivering the specific changes required, local authorities need to focus on developing their capacity to deal with continuous change. This requires:

- The development of the political process.

- A focus on strategic management rather than planning.

- Flexibility of structures and systems.

- Devolution of responsibility.

- Staff development and empowerment.

- Strong links with citizens, communities and users.

- A focus on learning.

Many of these themes will be picked up in later chapters. However the aim of this book is not to deal with a series of separate management topics, but to explore the idea of culture as the patterns of meaning which can turn initiatives like these into something with transformative power rather than something mechanistic to be complied with. An understanding of culture adds a new dimension to the rather mechanistic and structure oriented traditions of local government management. It can enrich and strengthen approaches to management, whether this is the day-to-day management of people or the process of large scale organisational transformation. But it needs to be an understanding which acknowledges some of the difficulties of the concept of culture itself. Chapter 2 begins by setting out an approach to understanding culture and explores the possibilities of cultural change.

CHAPTER REVIEW

This chapter has argued that:

- Local authorities face a series of challenges, in their role as deliverers of services and in their broader 'governance' role.

- These challenges require fundamental transformations of both internal and external relationships and patterns of authority.

- An understanding of culture is critical to both the management of change in local government, and to the process of political renewal.

- Multiple change agendas mean that local authorities need to focus on developing their cultural capacity for change, rather than just delivering specific initiatives.

■ Cultural change is more usefully thought of in terms of shaping and moulding new cultures rather than in terms of direct intervention and management.

2
Understanding culture

THIS CHAPTER:

- Reviews definitions of culture.

- Provides a framework for understanding the key features of culture.

- Highlights features of local government culture.

- Identifies some of the asumptions of the 'corporate culture' literature.

- Explores the problems and possibilities of cultural change.

Defining organisational culture

Culture has been defined in an alarmingly wide range of ways, making it a rather elusive idea to pin down. Culture has variously been defined as:

> ... the social glue that holds the organisation together (Baker 1980).

> ... how we do things around here (Ouchi 1981).

> ... a company's way of doing things (Deal and Kennedy 1982).

> ... a hidden yet unifying theme that provides meaning, direction and mobilisation (Kilmann et al. 1985).

> The culture of an organisation defines appropriate behaviour, bonds and motivates individuals and asserts solutions where there is ambiguity (Hampden-Turner 1990).

> 'Culture' refers to the underlying values, beliefs, and principles that serve as a foundation for an organisation's management system as well as the set of management practices and behaviours that both exemplify and reinforce those basic principles (Denison 1990).

> ... those mechanisms that organisational members use to attribute meaning to events (Sackmann 1991).

Culture represents an interdependent set of values and ways of behaving that are common in a community and that tend to perpetuate themselves, sometimes over long periods of time (Kotter and Heskett 1992).

There are some important differences of approach and emphasis here. One lies in the difference between the 'corporate culture' literature and the 'interpretive' literature. The former (Hampden-Turner 1990, Deal and Kennedy 1982, Peters and Waterman 1982, Kotter and Heskett 1992) define culture as a variable which can be manipulated in the same way that structures and systems can be managed. It is something which an organisation *has*, rather than something which an organisation *is*. A more interpretive approach is offered by Sackmann and others. This views culture as actively created by organisational members through their social interactions. It is not a separate variable but is deeply embedded in all aspects and processes of organisational life.

One interesting definition from the interpretive approach, which views culture as a 'web of understanding', is offered by McLean and Marshall:

> *Culture represents the understandings that we live by as members of an organisation; these are carried as symbols which act as vehicles for meaning. In addition to specific meanings, we also absorb other things characteristic of the culture such as attitudes and ways of thinking about the world. Culture is something that is lived, and the lived reality may not always coincide with statements about the culture. One image of culture is that it represents a web of understanding that we need in order to make sense of and cope with the complexity and confusion of organisational life. This web then gives shape to what we do and the ways in which we do it* (McLean and Marshall 1988 p. 11).

I will pick up some of the themes in this last definition – those of symbols, meanings, attitudes, understandings and lived practices – in the next chapter, and suggest how a local authority or department might understand its culture by exploring these different elements.

A framework for understanding culture

This section provides a framework for understanding culture which draws on the most salient features of a range of approaches and definitions. Culture can be viewed as:

Part of the informal organisation

Culture flows in and around the formal structures, systems and relationships within a local authority. It shapes, and is shaped by, how these formal processes actually work. For example, whether new structures give rise to new patterns of relationship and control, or how far they simply 'move the furniture around' and leave individuals doing much the same things as before, can be profoundly influenced by the culture. Because culture is part of the informal organisation, it requires different skills from the formal, rational processes which underpin other areas of management practice. It requires 'sensing' skills: the ability to see patterns in people's actions and interactions; the capacity to pick up jokes, gossip, and other informal communication processes; the ability to get a 'feel' for how things actually work and what evokes people's commitments and loyalties. Those with a good feel of the culture will be able to 'work' the informal as well as the formal organisational practices and channels.

Taken for granted

Culture is part of our everyday reality. It is what makes complex things – decisions, relationships, interactions with users – simple enough to deal with on an everyday basis because the culture we inhabit tells us how we should respond to routine events. But this very everyday, mundane, taken for granted quality means that it difficult to 'see' it once we are inside it. The first month or so in a new job, on joining a new team, on relocating to a different area, is when cultural learning is at its most acute. After that perceptions become muted and individuals become the unconscious transmitters of the culture to the next 'generation' of incomers.

A site of meaning

It is through the culture of an organisation, workgroup, department or profession that events are given meaning. Culture mediates understandings of the world, filters the complexity of everyday events, and helps shape view of what is important.

> *The organisation, otherwise an abstract bundle of concepts, is given meaning by its members who 'think' it in ways they have developed and learned* (Anthony 1994 p. 48).

A local authority's culture, then, acts as a filter through which events – anything from a new piece of legislation to a change of role or title of an individual job – are interpreted. And these interpretations shape how people respond and act. This is why communication of values and ideas is so important in cultural change: they help shape a common meaning system. For example is a mistake to be seen as an indicator of failure or something to be learned from? Is a restructuring to be seen as yet another exercise in cost cutting or as a means of devolving responsibility more effectively? Narratives, stories, face-to-face meetings between senior managers and front line staff, all help to shape the meanings which come to be embedded in the cultural currency of an organisation or group.

Evolutionary

Culture is learnt. It is passed on from generation to generation as an organisation evolves, changing gradually over time. One of the best descriptions of this process is that of Schien (1984), who defines culture as:

> ... the pattern of basic assumptions that a given group has invented, discovered or developed in learning to cope with its problems of external adaptation and internal integration, and that have worked well enough to be considered valid, and, therefore, to be taught to new members as the correct way to perceive, think, and feel in relation to those problems (Schien 1984, reprinted in Salaman (ed.) 1992).

Culture is like language: we inherit it, learn it, pass it on to others, but in the process we invent new words and expressions so that it evolves over time. Culture, like language, can only 'live' insofar as we use it: it is, then, part of subjective as well as objective reality. And culture, like language, is hard to control. One problem for local authorities trying to promote cultural change is the gap between the 'formal' socialisation process – through official communication channels, induction programmes, training and so on – and the informal socialisation processes which are present in every workplace.

Heterogeneous

Cultures are complex and layered. There is, then, a problem about talking of a *single* organisational culture. Meyerson and Martin (1987) distinguish between three approaches to studies of culture: the integrationist perspective; the differentiation perspective; and the fragmentation perspective (see box below). Each of these has something to offer to local authorities seeking to understand their organisations and manage change effectively.

THREE PERSPECTIVES ON CULTURE

Integrated

Portrays culture as organisation-wide, internally consistent, and consensual.

Differentiated

Portrays culture as differentiated into subcultures which are internally consistent within their boundaries but which coexist in harmony, conflict or indifference.

Fragmented

Sees cultures as internally inconsistent and as cross-cut with ambiguity. People may belong to multiple groups and have multiple loyalties not tied to a single subculture, and so not consistent with each other. Consensus and dissensus will coexist in fluctuating patterns depending on how events are interpreted.

Based on: Meyerson and Martin 1987; and Frost 1991

Local government have traditionally been strongly *differentiated* around departmental cultures with distinct power bases, values and professional practices. Meaning is likely to be primarily constructed within these subcultures, so that department or professional identity may well be stronger than organisational identity. In addition, administrative and professionally based cultures (for example the finance division and the social services department) see the world in different ways and speak different languages. Cultural divisions between and within departments or units are the source of potential lines of internal conflict.

There may also be deep divisions between the cultures of centre and periphery. Compare, for example, the cultural differences between a finance department and a service delivery unit; between the town hall and a neighbourhood office. This does not deny that each local authority will have elements of a shared culture deriving from its distinctive history and traditions. But change to this history and traditions will be patterned in different ways in specific departments, professions and functions.

But subcultures are not the only line of division. People belong to multiple groups and have multiple sets of loyalties and identities. Local authorities are characterised by the *intersection* of administrative, professional and bureaucratic, and now managerial, cultures, giving rise to multiple loyalties and identities within individuals. In this sense they can be understood as *fragmented* cultures. Each individual will have connections with multiple groups and alternative frameworks of meaning. For example an individual may belong to a professional culture, a project team group and to a specific business or service unit, as well as to the culture of the local authority as a whole. These may give rise to conflicting meanings and to dilemmas between different sets of priorities and injunctions. Individuals may also have loyalties to a local community culture and perhaps to a wider 'public service' culture, each of which may conflict with specific organisational goals. These different attachments will be activated as a result of how a specific event is interpreted. The culture is, then, never 'closed'. Indeed, if it were, the possibility of change or evolution would be closed.

Contested

It is misleading to view culture as sealed from and unaffected by the exercise of power, whether in party politics or organisational politics. Conflict is often played out through the mobilisation of cultural values and norms. For example there may be cultural conflict between those defending 'old' (public service or professional) values against 'new' (business or market-based) values. Ideas underpinning cultural change are often highly abstract: for example, the management ideas of 'business', 'quality', or the 'market'. Their very abstractness makes them ideal targets for struggles over meaning. In the case of 'quality' for example, managerial definitions (corporate standards), professional definitions (service improvement) and user definitions (perhaps greater power over decisions) all vie with each other for dominance.

Similarly, political ideas such as 'community', 'citizenship' and 'equal opportunities' are open to a multitude of interpretations. 'Devolution of power' and 'decentralisation' may, in particular, be interpreted differently by officers and members. Such concepts have no precise meaning, are owned by no particular group. The struggle to establish dominance of a particular domain often takes place through struggles over the meaning of words and ideas. For example, the idea of the 'enabling authority' has been through many different shifts, from Nicholas Ridley's minimalist conception of local government to Ranson and Stewart's view of the local authority's expansive role in 'enabling the learning society' (Ranson and Stewart 1994).

Cultural change, then, is likely to be a source of potential conflict and division as well as of consensus, amongst both members and officers. It is a site in which power bases are shifted and realigned as groups are mobilised to support or resist change, and as individuals learn the rhetoric of the new values. 'Resistance' can often be understood in terms of the defence of what used to be held as basic beliefs. Culture is also the site in which definitions of 'insiders' (guardians of the culture) and 'outsiders' (those who challenge accepted norms and values, or who do not 'fit' in terms of gender, race or other characteristics) are realigned – a process rife with conflict.

Dynamic

The notion of culture as evolutionary implies a natural or organic process of change. However, organisations cannot be treated as if they are sealed from their environment. The culture of a local authority will interact dynamically with its environment, being continuously shaped and reshaped through the cultural values, beliefs and norms which their members, users and staff bring from the outside world. These do not just reflect wider social cultures and cultural differences (including those of class, race, gender and age); they actively help to reproduce them. But more than this, the cultures within a particular local authority should positively reflect and interact with the cultures of the locality it serves in order to be *local* government.

The problems and possibilities of 'managing' culture

The literature on culture has provided a rich seam of imagery and metaphors, providing a new and very different perspective on the study and management of organisations. However, the excitement which has been generated has tended to lead to a search for simple prescriptions for change which can fit within existing imagery and frameworks. This has led to views of culture as an addition to the 'toolkit' of change management.

Problems in the culture literature

Much of the business literature on corporate culture is based on some rather dubious assumptions, of which I want to highlight four:

Assumption 1: cultures are integrated wholes

Organisations tend to be seen in terms of a single 'corporate culture' which is particular to an organisation, but relatively undifferentiated within it. This holistic picture is flawed since it does not encompass differentiation and diversity. The assumption is that this unified corporate identity can be imposed on an entire organisation:

... The current recipe is that a corporate culture can be created and imposed on a variety of individuals and groups, irrespective of their different interests, backgrounds, perspectives and different degrees of access to power (Anthony 1994 p. 97).

Assumption 2: cultures are closed societies

The anthropological tradition, on which the study of culture has drawn, derives from the study of closed, small scale groups or societies on which the outside world has little impact. Ethnographic methods – intensive, subjective immersion in one group over a lengthy period of time – are used to observe the rites, rituals, symbols, ceremonies, and unlocking their positive function in providing group cohesion and solidarity. In closed societies there is little access to alternative symbols or meaning systems. Modern organisations, however, interact dynamically with their external environment.

Assumption 3: cultures are 'consensual'

Concepts of culture draw heavily on models of organisations as organisms, in which all parts cooperate towards a common goal and where dysfunctional elements must be eliminated. The normal state is one of a natural equilibrium. based on harmony within the organisation, and harmony between the organisation and its environment. Conflict is viewed as unnatural, as a consequence of some communication defect which managers can 'fix' so that consensus can be restored.

This assumption heavily underplays the importance of competing values and interests, and is inadequate for conceptualising conflict and change. Nord comments:

> *When we consider these more complex organisations, the deficiencies in the conceptualisation of culture as glue become clear. The many parts of these systems are constantly changing, both themselves and in their relationships to each other. The existence of the larger entity depends as much on a dynamic tension among the parts as it does on their similarity .... Adequate conceptualisation of the bonding process that holds complex organisations together must be able to encompass repulsion as well as attraction; it must allow for changes in the parts; and it must treat the patterning among the parts (e.g. coalitions).* (Nord, Walter R. *Can organisational culture be managed?* in Frost et al. (eds) 1985).

Nord and others point to the inadequacy of texts which assume harmony is a 'natural' state and which neglect issues of power and resistance. The concept of culture, he argues, is often assumed to somehow stand apart from changes in structures, hierarchies, forms and patterns of control, and the distribution of resources. However, culture is a site in which competition between different and conflicting values is played out, and is a site of conflict over meanings.

Assumption 4: culture is a separate variable which can be managed

Meek, in her critique of the way in which theories from other disciplines are sometimes borrowed inappropriately by organisational theorists, suggests that:

> *The problem with some studies of organisational culture is that they appear to presume that there exists in a real and tangible sense a collective organisational culture that can be created, measured and manipulated in order to enhance organisational effectiveness* (Meek 1988 p. 453).

The reality of organisational life is more complex, and change is more dynamic, than such a 'cultural engineering' model might suggest. It is not possible to produce a 3-step (or even a 10-stage) programme for bringing about cultural change which will be effective whatever the context or whatever the problem to be addressed.

The dynamics of change

The model of culture set out in this chapter suggests that any programme of cultural change will be experienced unevenly across an organisation as it is contested, resisted and adapted. Three key issues which frequently arise in change programmes are:

Conflicting values

Change often brings with it challenges to existing values, whether these are espoused values of senior managers or the values which are deeply held by staff. For example current cycles of change bring with them potential conflict between 'professional' and 'business' values.

Uneven development

Organisational cultures are not uniform. Plural cultures give rise to a diversity of responses to change initiatives. Even where all parts of an organisation are engaged in the same form of change, rates of change will be uneven. This idea can aid understanding of the *variable success* of corporate initiatives across different cultural segments of an organisation. It presents severe challenges to the unitary models of organisations found in most of the literature on culture, and in much of the popular work on managing change.

Ambiguities and dilemmas

Change will usually challenge existing practices and values, and the tension between old and new ways of doing things may create management dilemmas and areas of uncertainty. For example there may be tension between the drive for flexibility and the need to retain bureaucratic controls; or between the new concern about accountability to customers and the traditional concern about accountability to local communities. Other areas of tension may arise between efficiency and equity; or between 'business' orientation and pubic service ethos. These dilemmas impose conflicting injunctions on both politicians, managers and front line staff. They have material and practical outcomes and so have consequences for the way individuals and groups respond to change.

The importance of culture in managing change

Many writers on culture argue for caution in considering the possibilities of cultural change. Schein introduces one of his key works with the comment:

> *Notice that I have not said 'manage the culture' because it is not clear whether that is possible or even desirable. But the consequences of culture are real, and these must be managed* (Schein 1985 xii).

While there are no quick fixes or easy solutions, change programmes are likely to be more effective if the managers involved have understood some of the basic features of the culture they are working in. The change itself is likely to be more embedded, ownership of the change is likely to be stronger, and staff will find it easier to adapt to and work with new conditions and practices if attention is paid to the cultural dimensions of change.

The next chapter begins by providing frameworks which managers and members might use to help in identifying the salient cultural features of the culture of their local authority.

CHAPTER REVIEW

This chapter has argued that:

- Culture has to be understood as part of the informal organisation, and is an important site of meaning and identity.
- Culture is heterogeneous, with different groups ascribing different meanings to their work and to the organisation as a whole.

- Culture is, then, the site of conflict and dilemmas as well as of integration and shared values.

- While there are some problems with the idea of culture as directly manageable, an understanding of culture will enhance management approaches, including the management of change.

3

Cultural analysis

THIS CHAPTER:

- Sets out a 'layered' model of culture.

- Identifies questions for exploring each layer.

- Provides a range of methods for analysing the cultures of a local authority, department or unit.

- Discusses the importance of cultural differentiation.

Cultural analysis is not an exact science. Because culture is concerned with 'webs of meaning' it is not readily accessible to the observer. How a local authority publicly presents itself – through its buildings, its publicity, and its general ethos – is immediately visible, but the everday norms and patterns of interaction (for example how staff interact with users, how informal reward mechanisms operate, how the officer/member relationship works) need more careful study. Yet others – the attitudes, values and beliefs – often only manifest themselves when challenged, for example by a programme of change.

Exploring the culture, then, means stripping away its different layers, like peeling the layers of an onion (Schien 1985). For simplicity, I use a three-layered model of culture which comprises *symbols, practices and values*.

Symbols (signals about what is important and valued in this organisation)

Cultural symbols play an important role in helping construct meaning. Language, artifacts, traditions, buildings and a host of other symbols act as 'carriers' of the culture and send signals about the values and practices which are appropriate. Symbols can be high profile (deliberately created) or low profile (part of the informal organisation).

High profile symbols

These include 'official' ceremonies and traditions; the physical environment; the public style and imagery through which the organisation interacts with the public. They are also to be found in the messages conveyed through deliberate channels of communication such as 'visions', 'missions', logos, slogans, publications, speeches, and corporate newspapers, reports, posters and publicity materials.

Low profile symbols

These include stories and moral tales, jokes, gossip, 'unofficial' communication channels, dress and appearance. They include how people 'customise' the physical environment as they use it, and the informal ceremonies and traditions which they create for themselves. Important messages about how to negotiate the informal organisation – how power works, how sexuality is managed, how mistakes are handled, how 'outsiders' are treated – are mostly conveyed through low profile symbols and the everyday language that is used to give meaning to events.

Practices (behaviour and action)

This is the element of culture that is expressed in the phrase 'how we do things around here' (Ouchi 1981). It includes routines, everyday patterns of interaction, how people spend their time, how they solve problems, how technology is used, how work is processed and so on. Practices include the 'official' behaviours sanctioned and held in place through formal structures, systems and management controls, but also the 'informal' practices sustained through group norms, customs and the everyday 'recipes' for problem solving and decision making that have evolved over time.

Values (deep structures of attitudes and beliefs)

We can distinguish here between 'espoused' values which the local authority talks about in its public pronouncements, and the 'embedded' values of staff, managers and members: their personal beliefs, their professional values, their political and community allegiances, and their identification or otherwise with 'public service' values.

The interaction between these layers is important. For example the culture of 'customer care' is conveyed by high profile symbols such as the style and design of reception areas, notices and leaflets, and low profile symbols such as the everyday dress and deportment of staff. It is expressed in the practices with which staff interact with the public: how queries or complaints are dealt with, how the telephone is answered, whether staff 'own' a problem or pass it on to someone else. Underpinning all of this is a set of values about the role of the local authority in serving the public and a perception of users as having rights and entitlements to be well treated. These must be reflected in the attitudes and practices of the whole organisation, not just of front line staff.

The next three sections provide some ways of exploring these different layers of culture. Each includes sets of questions which members, managers and staff can use to explore their culture, whether of their authority, department, unit or local office.

Reading the symbols

One way of exploring your culture is by studying the symbols. While it is not possible to 'read' an organisation's values and beliefs, and typical ways of doing things, from its symbols alone, they give important clues about what the organisation considers to be important, and are a very significant source of meanings for both staff and the wider community.

Reading the symbols: diagnostic questions

Buildings (the architecture, decor, style, colour, use of space)

— *What signals do you think these send to staff?*

— *What signals to you think these send to users?*

— *What signals do council chamber and meeting rooms convey about the expected style of political process?*

Style and imagery (through which the organisation interacts with the public)

— *What messages are conveyed by staff uniforms, facilities, notices, access for people with disabilities, types of barriers between staff and public, facilities for parents and children?*

— *What do these convey about what the organisation sees as important and unimportant?*

— *What messages are sent about the kind of relationships it seeks with different groups of users?*

The civic suite of local authority A is plush and hushed. The walls contain a series of portraits of past mayors, all in similar style and pose. The main feature of the foyer is a glass case in which ceremonial silverware is displayed. The committee rooms are laid out and decorated in a formal style.

The civic suite of local authority B is a public place, with rooms available for parties and weddings. The decor is bright and informal. A good deal of wall space is given over to public information, and there is currently a display of paintings from a local group. There is a small play area with children's toys, and tea/coffee machines for public and staff. There is usually a hum of activity going on.

Publicity materials and other communications

- Look at the logos, slogans, publications, speeches, job advertisements, forms, 'visions', 'missions' and other official communications.

- Explore the vocabulary and language used; the pictures, graphics and layout.

- What messages are they designed to convey?

- What do these tell you about the way in which the organisation wishes to be seen?

- What do they assume about the 'public'? Who is included and excluded?

When it looked at its publicity materials across all of its activities, one local authority found that when materials were addressed to paying customers (e.g. users of leisure centres) the pictures were of predominantly young white families, while when addressed to those dealing with people with 'needs' (e.g. users and carers of the social services department) they included more representations of people from black and ethnic minority groups, and of people with disabilities. Where publicity was directed to sponsors and stakeholders (e.g. the 'business community') the illustrations tended to be of white men in suits.

Staff

- Look at the way in which staff send signals about their relative degrees of friendliness, accessibility, and helpfulness.

- What does this say about the culture?

- What image does this create for the organisation?

Senior managers

- *What kinds of signals do they send to staff, and external stakeholders about what is valued in this organisation?*

- *What do they pay attention to?*

- *What kinds of behaviour do they model?*

- *What kind of style and ethos do they help create?*

- *How do they spend their time?*

One authority expects chief officers to spend regular time in front line offices and reception areas working alongside staff. Although it became evident to staff that senior managers could not necessarily 'do the job' very effectively, this activity was of enormous symbolic importance in giving recognition and value to front line services, and helped change previous sets of top down authority relations. It also gave senior managers a vital insight into the work of their department and the response of users.

Management practices

- *Look at how the last 'crisis' in the organisation was managed.*

- *Why was it called a crisis?*

- *What signals did the way it was managed send out?*

Ceremonies, traditions, 'heroes' and 'heroines'

- *Look at what gets celebrated, either officially or unofficially, and identify the 'heroes' or 'heroines' who are held in high regard. The organisation may well also have villains and scapegoats.*

- *What does this tell you about what is valued in this organisation?*

Status symbols

- *Identify formal and informal symbols of status, power and authority – office decor, allocation of car park spaces, access to secretarial support or the latest computer technology, private or open plan offices and so on.*

- *What does this tell you about power and hierarchy in your organisation?*

One department felt it had made great progress in eradicating status divisions by introducing flatter hierarchies, by allocating car park spaces according to job requirements, and by eradicating differentials of office size and style by moving to open plan offices. However a culture workshop with staff revealed that informal status divisions between different local offices were rife, based on a (long abandoned) practice of using postings to 'difficult' areas as an informal sanction. Being allocated to one particular local office was still seen by staff in terms of being 'sent to Siberia'. Working at the centre, in contrast, was seen as a reward and incentive.

Jokes, gossip and stories

- *What are the 'morals' which these convey to the listeners?*

- *How does the grapevine work?*

Stories about sex and relationships are rife in most organisations. What is less well understood is that these stories often carry messages about how sexuality is to be managed in a work environment.

Language

- *Listen to the language used. How is this changing?*

One exercise is to ask a group of staff or managers to write new bits of language that have started being used in the organisation over the last few years on separate 'postits' and to then group these into themes by rearranging them on a wall. This can highlight the ways in which different ideas are becoming embedded in the culture, and perhaps even suggest an overall cultural shift.

- *How inclusive or exclusive is the language?*

Language is universally acknowledged to be an important element of culture. It is through language that we construct and come to share meanings. The identity of an organisation, or other cultural grouping (profession, departmental, social) is demarcated through the use of distinct language, the meaning of which is only understood by insiders. The use of one of these 'insider' languages (for example technical or professional languages) often involves relationships of power with outsiders.

Exploring behaviours and practices

Decoding the symbols is not enough on its own. Culture is expressed and reproduced through people's everyday behaviours, practices and interactions.

Exploring behaviours and practices: diagnostic questions

Use of time

- *How do people spend their time? (in or out of offices, talking or writing, in meetings, in contact with users, walking about and so on).*

Communication

- *How do people communicate with each other? (in writing, by phone, by visiting each other, through computer technology and so on).*

- *What are the main formal and informal communication channels?*

- *Do the main patterns of information flow mainly downwards?*

- *How much information really comes up the organisation?*

- *How good is the communication across departmental or divisional boundaries?*

- *How does the organisation communicate with members?*

- *What are the main communication barriers and biases?*

Interaction with the public

- *What actually happens in reception areas?*

- *What happens if you sample the service as a user?*

- *What are the processes through which an enquiry or complaint is handled, and how effective are they from the public's point of view?*

Interaction between officers and members

- *Are there informal as well as formal occasions to discuss policy issues?*

- *How are members kept informed?*

- *How are members given support in their role in representing their ward?*

- *Do members communicate only with chief officers or have they access directly to staff responsible for a particular area of work?*

Working practices

- *How effective are the processes through which work is handled on a day-to-day basis?*

- *What procedures are used, and are these still relevant?*

- *How effectively do people work in teams?*
- *How effective is the use of Information Technology?*

Performance measures

- *Are staff told what is expected?*
- *What behaviours are encouraged by the performance indicators used to measure the effectiveness of a particular team or unit?*
- *Do they focus on what is really important?*
- *What kinds of rewards are in place?*
- *How are members involved in monitoring and reviewing performance?*

Systems

- *What kinds of incentives are set through budgeting and other systems?*
- *Do they reward an increase in inputs (e.g. more 'cases' to be dealt with) or outputs (results delivered)?*
- *Do they reward keeping to budget limits; or using financial resources effectively in order to provide 'value for money'?*
- *Do financial management systems help or hinder the devolution of financial management?*
- *Do the systems established by central departments support greater flexibility and business orientation within units?*
- *Do systems support or hinder community involvement?*

Surfacing values and attitudes

Values and attitudes can only really be identified through the use of qualitative techniques (interviews, discussions, focus groups, workshops) which are discussed in the next section. Some of the dimensions which are important in a local government context include beliefs about users; stereotypes about particular groups of users or staff; assumptions about other departments or professions; assumptions about particular communities; attitudes to business goals, contract management and partnership working; and values about service goals and equality issues.

Surfacing values and attitudes: diagnostic questions

– *What public or community values are held to be important?*

– *What beliefs about users are held by staff?*

For example are users seen as 'unreasonable/reasonable', as 'demanding of, or entitled to', the service concerned; as essentially honest or dishonest?

– *What beliefs and stereotypes are held about particular groups?*

For example about people with disabilities; older people; people from black and ethnic minority groups; people who live in particular areas or estates?

– *What beliefs and stereotypes are held about particular categories of staff?*

For example about women managers; part time staff; staff with disabilities; manual or clerical staff; staff who work on a contract or agency basis?

– *What beliefs and stereotypes are held by officers about councillors?*

... and by councillors about officers?

– *What kinds of cross-departmental or team attitudes are prevalent?*

Are these competitive or collaborative; combative or cooperative?

– *What kinds of attitudes do service staff hold about the corporate centre?*

... and do central departments hold about service units?

– *What kinds of beliefs about 'partner' organisations in the private, voluntary or statutory sectors are held?*

What is the prevailing view about how inclusive or exclusive, arm's length or collaborative, these relationships should be?

– *What kinds of attitudes to contract management seem to have emerged?*

For example arm's length, hard nosed, relational, problem solving?

– *What are the attitudes which underpin relationships between managers and staff?*

How open and democratic, or authoritative and distanced, are these thought to be?

– *What basic orientations to change do different groups of staff express?*

33

Using the questions

These questions can be used in both formal and informal approaches to cultural analysis. They can be used to suggest fruitful subjects to explore through direct observation or group discussions. They can also be used to suggest questions for surveys or questionnaires. One way of doing this is to turn the questions you are most interested in into statements, with respondents being asked to indicate how far they agree or disagree with each statement, with some space to write additional comments. For example, if you were interested in exploring the final questions listed above – on orientations to change – you might structure this as follows:

Staff in this department generally welcome change

Strongly agree   Tend to agree   Tend to disagree   Strongly disagree

☐   ☐   ☐   ☐

Please note any comments below:
_____
_____

The questions I have suggested are intended as illustrative rather than exhaustive. It is hoped that you will use them to develop the questions that are of most relevance to the context of a particular local authority. The following chapter – on typologies of culture – may well suggest others. First, however, I want to explore a range of diagnostic techniques.

Diagnostic techniques

This section offers a range of qualitative and quantitative techniques, then pulls these together into a systematic methodology of cultural analysis.

Observation

The simplest approach to analysing the culture is based on direct observation of the symbols and practices, the patterns of behaviour and relationships, that are evident to you as a 'participant observer' (i.e. as a member of the organisational group). Being a participant observer requires you to put yourself at a distance from the culture you are immersed in for the moment so that you can stand back, listen and watch. You may wish to involve someone else from outside the immediate culture in order to bring a sharper spotlight on what you yourself have come to take for granted.

Observation can take place at almost any time – in meetings, in informal gatherings, looking at how users are dealt with, moving around the building and looking at informal patterns of behaviour and interaction, listening to jokes and gossip and so on. This will give you clues rather than a systematic analysis; but clues are often very revealing of emerging issues or problems. To go beyond clues, however, something more is needed. Observations need to be checked out through a more systematic approach. This can still be small scale and simple; for example, by getting a group of staff and/or members to talk about the culture and how it responds to particular problems or challenges.

If you are a newcomer, if you wish to research cultures to which you do not have direct access, or if you wish to explore the whole local authority or departmental culture, a still more systematic approach is required. Observation remains important and is a rich source of data on the objective, tangible dimensions of culture, especially the high profile symbols. But you will need something which gives a check on the more subjective dimensions of culture:

- What the symbols mean to insiders.

- Why the behaviours and practices are done in this way.

- What the values and attitudes are which sustain the present culture.

- How users experience the service relationships.

- How external communities and groups perceive the culture of the organisation.

Staff surveys

An increasingly common technique of cultural analysis is the use of attitude surveys. The 'Investors in People' initiative has led to much more widespread use of staff surveys, and where these are skillfully constructed and sensitively administered they can be very valuable tools. To be effective, however, two requirements must be met. Firstly, the questions asked need to do more than ask about the issues you already know about, but must reflect issues which are likely to become more significant as your local authority attempts to respond to the challenges it faces. 'Off the peg' surveys may be less than

35

useful. Secondly, surveys may raise staff expectations that concerns which they express will be addressed, and managers must be prepared to make some visible changes as a result of the findings.

The hardest parts of any survey are firstly arriving at the right questions, and secondly decoding and using the results. The very nature of a formal survey means that it is difficult to ask follow-up questions or to check the meaning of particular responses once they have been made. For these reasons, surveys are best linked to more qualitative approaches based on interviews, workshops or focus groups.

Diagnostic interviews

Interviews with staff at different levels can reveal a richer cultural picture than the quantitative data gathered through surveys. As with surveys, interviews should be designed around the issues of most concern to a particular local authority or department, but might include some of the following.

Analysing your culture; interview or discussion questions

- *What words would you use to describe the culture you work in?*
- *What is important about its history? How does this influence the way it works today?*
- *What do you think gets rewarded in this culture?*
- *What are the strengths and weaknesses of this culture?*
- *How well does it handle change?*
- *How does it help or hinder the organisation's strategic goals?*
- *How resilient is it?*
- *How does it respond to new perspectives or ideas from within?*
- *How welcoming is it to 'outsiders' (marginalised groups)?*

Working with groups

The analysis of culture in discussion or focus groups draws on anthropological approaches. The focus is on identifying the symbols which the group sees as important, and then decoding the meanings which these symbols hold for group members. This often requires a bringing together of 'insiders' and 'outsiders', with a facilitator or consultant helping insiders to identify the symbols and practices which are important, and working with them to decode them. In such exercises it is important to distinguish between the creative or brainstorming stage, which aims to collect data, capturing fragments of cultural symbolism, and the analytical stage, which explores their meaning. The latter involves sustained work of cultural 'reading', digging behind the symbol itself to reveal the values and assumptions which it represents. Different elements of culture need to be explored in order to build up a pattern in which readings can be checked for consistency. Where inconsistencies arise, this may be a problem of 'misreading' some cultural clues, or it may signify a more complex cultural picture in which dilemmas and tensions need to be further explored. Two trigger techniques are outlined below: storytelling and drawing.

The storytelling exercise

Each member of a group is asked to recall a story which they were told when they joined the organisation or moved to a new department or team; or to think of a story which they themselves tell to new staff. They are asked to share their story with a partner from within the group, whose role it is to help the teller decode the 'moral' of the story. The morals (but not the stories) are then shared with the whole group and a discussion takes place about how far they reflect important aspects of the informal culture of the organisation.

Drawing the culture

Another technique is based on individuals or groups producing images of their organisation, in collages or sketched on flipchart paper. Imagery varies widely, but examples have included:

- A garden in which some parts were flourishing and others were dying (indicating morale problems in areas which felt neglected by the centre and starved of resources).

- Crumbling castles (indicating the welcome demise of previous departmental power bases and chief officer fiefdoms).

- The dangers of a wild wood (indicating exposure to new risks and hazards of the marketplace).

- The headless peacock (indicating new glowing corporate imagery accompanied by poor strategic thinking).

- The ship being tossed at sea with captain facing in the wrong direction and about to be swept overboard (indicating a sense of weak leadership at the top).

GLAMOROUS IMAGE

STUNTED ↓ GROWTH

← Thrashing about → limbs being chopped off

The local authority octopus

Text within the illustration:

WARNING!

DANGER
WICKED
WOOD

PUBLIC WORKS
FOREST.

HAZY PATH — HAVE TO KNOW IT.
ALL DRAWN BY SEARCH FOR REWARD (the Gingerbread house)
FRIGHTENED ANIMALS / PEOPLE
SHADOWY
HAUNTED BY GHOSTS OF PAST
BUT SECURITY — BECAUSE IT'S WHAT YOU KNOW
— AND THERE'S A BULLDOZER APPROACHING

The wild wood

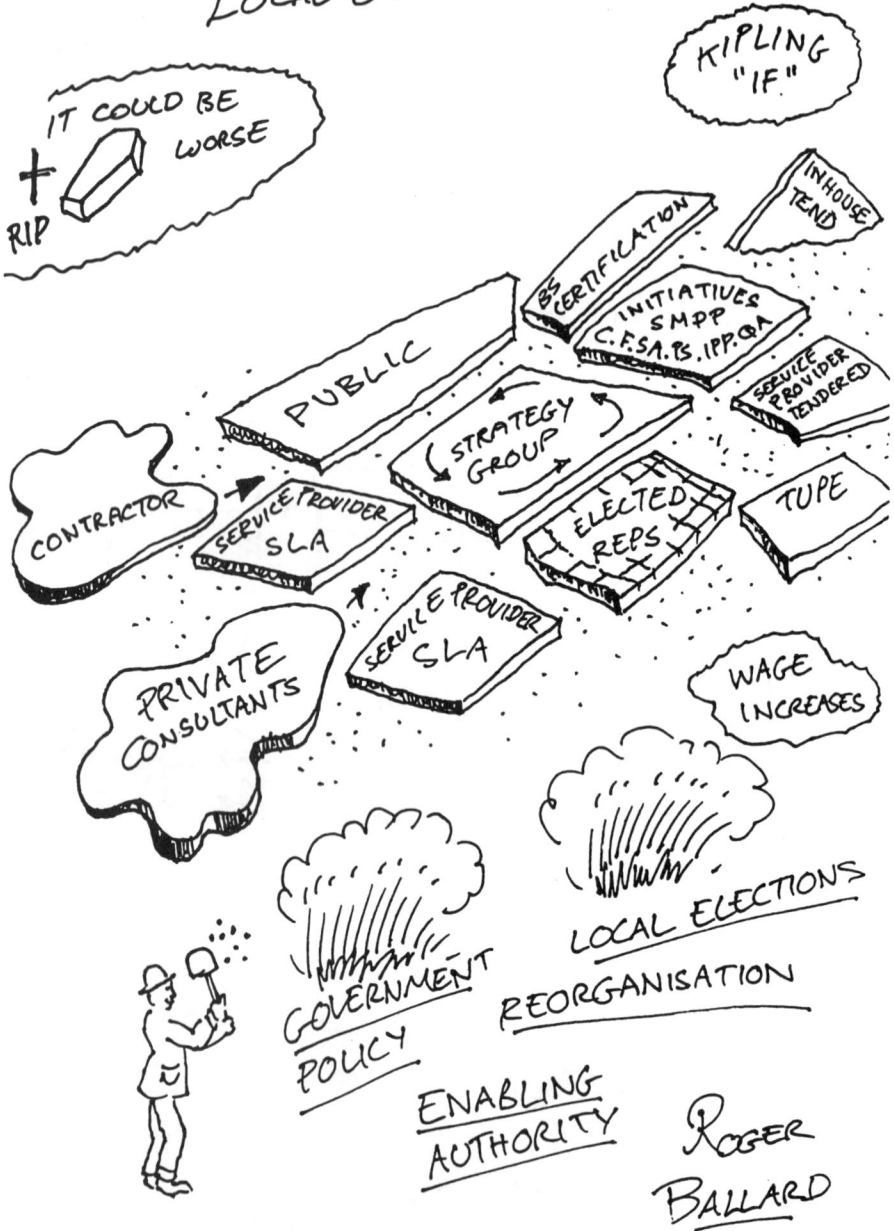

THE THEORY OF
PLATE TECHTONICS IN
LOCAL GOVERNMENT

KIPLING "IF."

IT COULD BE WORSE

+ RIP

INHOUSE TEND

BS CERTIFICATION

INITIATIVES SMPP
C.F.SA.BS.IPP.QA

PUBLIC

STRATEGY GROUP

SERVICE PROVIDER TENDERED

CONTRACTOR

SERVICE PROVIDER SLA

ELECTED REPS

TUPE

PRIVATE CONSULTANTS

SERVICE PROVIDER SLA

WAGE INCREASES

GOVERNMENT POLICY

LOCAL ELECTIONS

REORGANISATION

ENABLING AUTHORITY

Roger BALLARD

Tectonic plates (indicating new lines of fragmentation with parts grating against each other, the whole being fanned by the flames of government legislation).

Putting it together

The most productive approach is one based on four stages of cultural analysis.

THE FOUR STAGES OF CULTURAL ANALYSIS

Stage one

Identifies the most important questions to examine. This will usually emerge from discussions of the problems and challenges faced by the organisation and the cultural characteristics which might be necessary in the future.

Stage two

Attempts to gather qualitative information through a mix of observation, interviews and discussions with different staff groups.

Stage three

Checks out emerging themes and issues through a more systematic and representative staff survey. The survey questions are designed around the themes elicited during stage 2, perhaps drawing on some of the dimensions discussed in the next section to provide a framework for the questions.

Stage four

Looks at the results of the survey through a series of focus groups (perhaps based on some of the groups used in stage 2). The purpose of this stage is to both check and feed back the outcomes of the research and explore the implications for future change.

Exploring cultural differentiation

An important element of cultural analysis is concerned with exploring differentiation within organisations. The bureaucratic histories of most local authorities mean that functional or departmental boundaries are fairly strong, and it is not unusual to be able to identify the existence of well defended 'fiefdoms' with strong internal loyalty and well developed power maintenance strategies. These can be seen as organisational subcultures (and occasionally as counter cultures). Subcultures can also, of course, form around particular teams or activities (formal or informal). Social and other 'unofficial' subcultures may cross-cut those of the formal organisation, and these intersections are important for understanding the workings of power and the forming of alliances.

Subcultural differences help promote understanding of lines of conflict and sources of power within organisations. They can also suggest why general developments can be met with active resistance, or at best adopted unevenly across an organisation. Fig. 3.1 illustrates some of the cultural tensions between the corporate centre and a service team:

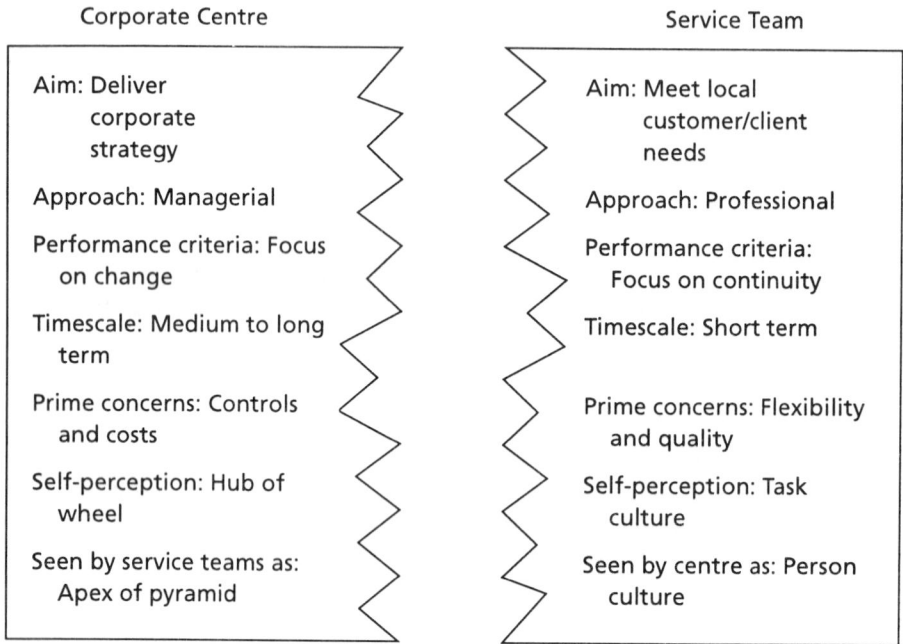

Corporate Centre	Service Team
Aim: Deliver corporate strategy	Aim: Meet local customer/client needs
Approach: Managerial	Approach: Professional
Performance criteria: Focus on change	Performance criteria: Focus on continuity
Timescale: Medium to long term	Timescale: Short term
Prime concerns: Controls and costs	Prime concerns: Flexibility and quality
Self-perception: Hub of wheel	Self-perception: Task culture
Seen by service teams as: Apex of pyramid	Seen by centre as: Person culture

Figure 3.1   Cultural tensions

The dynamics of power within an organisation can be linked to the interplay of different cultures within it. Ita O'Donovan suggests that current changes in local government have led to a greater differentiation of cultures as local authorities have become more fragmented.

The breaking down of monolithic departments into discrete units has meant that within these units we increasingly find a culture that is task-oriented with a greater emphasis on a team approach. Culture clash can occur between the new units and their core departments if the core is still strongly operating from a role perspective. This clash can be mirrored again between the core of service departments and the core of the authority when it is seeking to ensure corporate action across the authority as a whole (O'Donovan 1994 p. 15).

She uses Handy's typology (which I discuss in the next chapter) to suggest some of the differing patterns of behaviour that may emerge as follows:

Diverse responses to the changing environment of local authorities

(*Source:* O'Donovan 1994).

Staff operating in newer units may have:

- a sense of urgency; a need to have a response immediately;
- a feeling of threat: only they are exposed;
- a positive expression of enjoying the pace and 'being out in the world';
- a feeling of pride in the unit achievements;
- a frustration with the parent department and the core of the authority;
- an obsession with costs, quality and customers;
- a feeling of isolation;
- a concern that other units are not operating to the same rules.

Staff in the core of the authority may have:

- an awareness of being part of a new, leaner core, and consequently support for the service emphasis;
- a concentration on strategic direction, characterised by the need to communicate across the authority;
- a concern that fragmentation means loss of overall objectives;
- a feeling of defensiveness about the costs of the core;
- an inability to understand the emphasis on costs;
- an obsession with providing a quality service to the operational units;
- a wish to be appreciated;
- a concern with probity;

- a concern with corporate values;

- a concern for the authority to operate in particular areas as one organisation.

Staff in core service departments may have:

- a concern with departmental objectives and values;

- a concern with policy initiatives and guidelines;

- a concern for monitoring and evaluation of the operational units;

- a wish to maintain a distance from the core of the authority;

- a wish to decide for themselves when to cooperate and when to compete;

- a pride in their operational units;

- an obsession with providing support to their operational units.

This kind of analysis can lead to a recognition of contradictions or tensions resulting from the interplay of different cultures within a local authority. The following chapter provides frameworks for mapping cultures and cultural differences.

CHAPTER REVIEW

Cultural analysis is an important part of the managerial repertoire of change. Any change initiative will be enhanced if it is based on an understanding of the existing culture of your local authority, and of the departments and units which comprise it. In setting out techniques and approaches, this chapter has argued that:

- In analysing culture it is vital that the different 'layers' (symbols, practices and values) are explored.

- Analysis is likely to be more effective if both qualitative and quantitative techniques are used. A four stage process of systematic cultural analysis was suggested.

- Cultural analysis must take account of cultural differentiation within a local authority.

4

Mapping the culture

THIS CHAPTER:

- Identifies how cultural typologies can be used in cultural analysis.

- Sets out ten dimensions of local authority culture which can be used to map cultural strengths and weaknesses.

- Illustrates how 'cultural mapping' can be used to plot desired changes.

The approaches to cultural analysis set out in Chapter 3 were designed to explore the richness and complexity of a culture. This chapter goes on to look at how *cultural typologies* can help you to pull out particular cultural features and use these to highlight possible strengths and weaknesses. This will inform an understanding of how your culture might help or hinder you in managing particular problems or engaging in strategic change. It is only if you know where you are that you can identify how you need to go about getting to where you want to be.

Typologies of culture

Many writers (Deal and Kennedy 1982, Miles and Snow 1978, Ouchi 1980, Hofstede 1991) provide frameworks for classifying organisational cultures. Rather than exploring what is unique about a culture, typologies help identify what characteristics it shares with others due to similar environmental factors or historical developments. However the process of classifying is about simplifying the culture rather than revealing its richness and diversity. The danger is that any process of simplification may well leave important things out.

Shaping organisational cultures in local government

<u>CULTURAL FEATURES HIGHLIGHTED IN TYPOLOGIES</u>

Deal and Kennedy   Degree of risk taking.
Speed of feedback on actions.

Miles and Snow   Defenders and prospectors.

Ouchi   Culture of bureaucracy (segmented, rule bound).
Market culture (fluid, flexible and fast).
Clan culture (based around a product or service).

Charles Handy's typology is one of the most pertinent to public sector organisations because of their traditional combination of person (professional), power (political) and role (bureaucratic) cultures, and because of the current attempts to introduce task (results oriented) cultures. Handy's four cultures are:

Power culture (image: spider's web)

■ Central, powerful leader.

■ Widening circles of power and influence which cross-cut formal lines of authority.

■ Few rules; decisions made quickly.

■ Personal style, direct intervention.

■ Short lines of communication; little in writing.

■ Leaders rather than managers.

Typical organisation: small business based on a single entrepreneur.

In local government: often found in political party groups; central groups of chief executive and chief officers.

Role culture (image: Greek temple with vertical columns)

■ Based on roles rather than personalities.

■ Communication formalised.

- Lots of procedures, handbooks and rules.

- Managed rather than led.

- Provides equity of treatment.

Typical organisation: the traditional civil service bureaucracy.

In local government: traditionally found in most service departments, though many of these are attempting to change. However a role culture is still appropriate for many functions where standardisation and control are important.

Task culture (image: a net, with both horizontal and vertical connections between individuals)

- Project oriented, with groups coming together around tasks.

- Not much hierarchy.

- Team leaders rather than managers the key.

- Organised around plans not procedures.

- High levels of flexibility: task groups form and re-form as the needs of the organisation change.

Typical organisation: research company; consultancy firm.

In local government: increasingly popular, for example in project work and task groups. Usually operates within a role culture at the points where innovation, flexibility and fast responses are most needed.

Person culture (image: stars in a constellation)

- Individual expertise comes first (highly valued, highly paid).

- Organisation a resource to support the individual experts or professionals.

- Administrators have lower status than professionals.

Typical organisation: GP group practice or lawyers' chambers.

In local government: rare, though may be found in legal departments, training divisions and other forms of in-organisation consultancy.

Dominant culture	How change occurs	Change strategies
POWER	External forces	Know informal networks
	Change of personnel	Get to the leader
	Coup	Ignore procedures
	Growth	Watch your back
WORKING AT THE INTERFACE	*Learn to work with formal and informal power*	
ROLE	Restructure	Write report
	New posts	Bid for resources
	New procedures	Work through proper channels
WORKING AT THE INTERFACE	*Get round blocks by looking for power cultures Use project teams for flexibility*	
TASK	Scan environment to define problems	Enable people to work in flexible ways
	Set up new teams	Manage complex relationships
	Absorb results	
WORKING AT THE INTERFACE	*Collaborate across formal channels Work with multiple success criteria*	
PERSON	Change by agreement	Persuasion
	Change of personnel	Consensus building
	New environment (market or legislative)	Setting targets
WORKING AT THE INTERFACE	*Work with both professional and managerial goals and skills*	

Figure 4.1 Situational strategies

Each of these has implications for decision-making processes within a local authority both as an organisation and as a political institution. Power cultures are found within both member and senior officer groups, and in many community based organisations. Because decision-making tends to be closed and fast, acccess and participation are difficult. The formality of the role culture, although much maligned in critiques of local authorities as

bureaucracies, does ensure probity and accountability through cl
rules and procedures. Task cultures potentially open out decisio
enable a local authority to draw on a range of insights and skills ..
organisation, and sometimes beyond it. Accountability may, however, be less
clear, and both members and public may be more comfortable dealing with an
individual rather than a team, however effectively its members work together.

Handy's four cultures also give rise to different kinds of change strategies and
practices. Figure 4.1 on page 48 sets out how each culture deals with change,
and some of the implications for those working across more than one culture.

Dimensions of culture

The problem with typologies of culture, including that of Handy, is that they
don't take you very far. If, for example, you think your local authority is a role
culture studded here and there by task cultures, overarched by a power
culture of lead members and chief officers, where does this take you next?
What specific elements should you attempt to change?

A rather richer and more detailed way of exploring cultural differences is to
plot a culture not as one of four 'types' but along a series of dimensions of
cultural difference expressed in a series of continua (e.g. centralised/
decentralised). This enables you to think then about where your local
authority might be on the continuum (too centralised, too decentralised, or
tensions between the two as a result of inconsistent policies) and what specific
changes might be needed. The 'top ten' dimensions which I have found most
useful in local authority settings are:

DIMENSIONS OF CULTURE: THE TOP TEN

Process oriented.	Results oriented.
Moralist.	Pragmatist.
Open.	Closed.
Managerial.	Professional.
Loose.	Tight.
User/community driven.	Producer driven.
Uniformity valued.	Diversity valued.
Reactive.	Proactive.
Centralised.	Decentralised.
Hierarchical.	Democratic.

Some of these dimensions draw on Hofstede (1991), but they have been reshaped and augmented for a local government context, being largely drawn from workshops with local government managers. Each is explained and discussed below.

Process oriented/results oriented

In a *process oriented culture* what matters is *how* you do things. This means following the proper procedures, whether this concerns issues of probity and accountability, or ensuring that certain values (e.g. community involvement or consultation) are put into practice in decision-making processes. A culture which is strongly process oriented is likely to value the representational and policy roles of members, and to ensure that all decision-making goes through 'proper channels' rather than being short circuited. A process oriented culture tends to avoid risk and to be slow paced. It will view accountability in terms of whether the processes through which decisions are made are correctly followed.

A *results oriented culture*, in contrast, is less concerned with how things are done than with what is achieved. It is task based and fast paced. 'Correct' decision-making processes may be short circuited – there may not be time to consult everyone or to wait for the next committee cycle. This means that risks have to be tolerated to a greater extent. This culture will view accountability in terms of whether the outcomes are in line with the goals and policies which are being pursued.

Process oriented	Results oriented
How we do things is important.	What we achieve is important.
Risk avoiding.	Risks accepted.
Slow paced.	Fast paced.
Accountability for the processes by which decisions are made	Accountability for outcomes.

What matters to a local authority is where each of these cultures is most appropriate, and whether it has the overall balance right. For example a personnel department may need to retain strong elements of process orientation in order to comply with equality policies. A team putting together a city challenge bid or preparing a unit for CCT will need to have strong elements of results orientation. A personnel department facing CCT needs both!

Moralist/pragmatist

A moralist culture has a strong basis of values. The values may be political values (democracy, participation, community empowerment), professional values (responding to client needs) or managerial values (high quality services to customers, caring for staff). Equality goals may cut across all three. What matters is that the values are lived out in the way in which the local authority pursues its activities – it sticks to its beliefs. Change programmes also tend to be value driven.

A pragmatist culture does whatever is necessary to get the job done. The language is more likely to be one of objectives and targets. Change programmes tend to be built around a series of short term initiatives.

Moralist	Pragmatist
We stick to our beliefs.	We do whatever is necessary to get the job done.
Strong organisational values.	Weak organisational values.
Value driven change processes.	Focus on planning and implementation.

Local authorities need to draw on both of these, depending on the issues it faces. Its traditions mean that a foundation of public service values is important. Current managerial thinking also suggests that value driven change is more likely to be effective than a series of short term pragmatic initiatives. However the requirements to cut costs and to focus on efficiency above all else can produce a shift towards pragmatism. It is the balance between these that is important.

Open/closed

A closed culture has strong organisational boundaries and weak internal and external networks. Communities are kept at a distance, and parts of the organisation which have, by necessity, close contact with a local community tend to be marginalised. There is little user involvement. There may be token consultation excercises with users or communities but little is done with the results. Partnerships may have been developed but again these are marginalised, and tend to be viewed as a necessary evil rather than a positive source of innovation and opportunity.

An open culture has weaker boundaries and values its internal and external networks. It is open to new ideas and welcomes opportunities for collaboration and joint working with external agencies. Multi-disciplinary and cross-departmental working is common. Users and communities are actively involved in shaping policies and services. Staff are likely to be involved in external activities through secondments, placements and work with community and voluntary groups. This is more likely to be a culture in which learning takes place.

Open	Closed
Weak boundaries.	Strong boundaries.
Strong internal and external networks.	Weak internal and external networks.

The current trend in local government is towards more open cultures, with higher degrees of user and community involvement and the growth of partnerships and multi-agency activities. It is, however, difficult to achieve this across a local authority as a whole. It may well take place at the very top with senior managers and chief executive involved in external networks and strategic partnerships. It may well also take place at local offices and front line services, where contact with communities and users is at its strongest. Central services and service departments as a whole may, however, retain predominantly closed cultures: networks here may well be professional rather than local. It is the interaction between these cultures – between, say, a neighbourhood office and an engineers' department – which is critical in the capacity of the local authority as a whole to engage in real learning.

Managerial/professional

This axis concerns how people view their work, and concerns their primary sources of loyalty and identity. In a *professional culture* there will be a primary identification with professional values, and the first loyalties will be to the profession as a whole and to the individual clients served. The language is likely to be one of clients, services, needs, problems, cases and case loads. Hierarchies are likely to operate around levels of experience and expertise. There will be an emphasis on gaining professional qualifications. In a *managerial culture* there will be a primary identification with the needs of the organisation. The language is likely to be one of strategies, objectives, performance, and costs. Hierarchies are likely to operate around contribution to the organisation's mission, with financial and strategic roles predominant. Management development – especially corporate management programmes – will be seen as more important than professional training except at junior levels.

Managerial	Professional
Strong identification and loyalty to organisation.	Strong identification and loyalty to profession.
Organisational hierarchies.	Expertise hierarchies.
Managerial language.	Professional language.
Management development.	Professional training.

This dimension has become more and more important as a result of recent cycles of public sector change towards managerial cultures. The process gives rise to considerable tensions, with some professions (especially in the National Health Service) strongly defending professional cultures, and others (including social services departments) becoming more and more managerial. The process affects voluntary as well as statutory organisations, and the shift from direct funding to contractual relationships with voluntary groups often leads to cultural change within them. In general exposure to the market and competitive pressures, the devolution of financial management and the setting up of business units all tend to increase the pace of change towards managerial cultures.

Loose/tight

This dimension is about the 'culture of control' within a department or unit. A *loose culture* will mean that people are largely responsible for their own work, and the amount of effort they put in. There may be a low concern for costs, and people are likely to be relaxed about time (meetings are unlikely to begin on schedule). People will tend not to be tied to their desks. Management information will be hard to come by. A *tight culture*, on the other hand, will be highly cost conscious. There is likely to be a strong emphasis on setting targets and measuring performance. Time itself will be viewed as a commodity and its use closely monitored. A great deal of management information will be generated (indeed in some cases too much to be of value).

Loose	Tight
Low concern for costs.	Cost conscious.
People largely responsible for their own effort levels.	Strong performance management.
	Tight control over time.
Loose control over time.	Possible excessive management
Poor management information.	information.

It is evident that the current context of local government means a shift from 'loose' to 'tighter' is needed. Many areas of activity in which people have in the past been trusted to get on with it – for example in professional services such as architecture or design – are introducing time recording and stronger performance management systems. The current interest in the management of sickness absence is also in line with a general cultural tightening in order to reduce costs. However a loose culture is appropriate in some contexts: for example a highly motivated project team engaged in some form of innovation. It is not possible to control people tightly since the nature of the task is itself unclear. It may be necessary to spend more than originally envisaged to get the desired result. It is difficult to generate precise measures of process performance, though it will be important to review the final outcome with considerable care and draw out 'process' lessons as part of the evaluation.

There are also dangers associated with introducing too much tightness. The result may be an impoverished culture in which people feel they are only valued for the precise and measured contribution they make, and may adjust their effort levels downwards as their commitment to a wider sense of purpose falls. Care is needed in evaluating which aspects of working practices require greater tightness, and leaving some room for manoeuvre elsewhere.

User or community driven/producer driven

This dimension refers to how far the design and delivery of services is driven by the needs and requirements of the organisation itself, and how far they have genuinely been transformed around the needs and requirements of users or communities. For example, one local authority identified its leisure facilities as towards the 'user driven' end of the spectrum in that it had high levels of consultation on what these should provide and how they should be designed. They had also established a number of user groups of each facility. Their IT section at the centre, however, was perceived as 'producer driven' in that users of the service perceived it to be inaccessible and unresponsive, and

felt that the section was more interested in their relationships ~
and in designing whole new systems than in ensuring that soft
tailored to the needs of particular users.

User driven	Producer driven
Driven by user needs.	Driven by needs of organisation.
High community involvement.	Low community involvement.

This dimension raises two interesting issues about the power relationships between producers and users, and between the local authority and its communities. Firstly, is it the case that where users have real choice, and can express their views through some kind of market (as in the case of the leisure facilities) producers are more prepared to change? Clearly not, since many parts of a local authority where there is little capacity for user choice are making great strides in consulting with users and communities. However, many are also reluctant. The second issue concerns how effective such involvement is. It may well be that the IT section in the authority quoted feels that it genuinely does attempt to seek user views in the design of software, but that users often don't know what they want or don't express it very well. The power of expertise and the power of language are clearly an issue here.

Similar, though not identical, issues are involved in community involvement exercises. These may range from token consultation to a genuine devolution of decision-making power. But even when the intention is the latter, the procedures, jargon and informal power of the local authority may impede the effectiveness of the efforts, however unintentionally.

Uniformity/diversity

This is closely related to the user or community driven/producer driven dimension. A *culture of uniformity* tends to assume that everyone is to be treated equally and has similar patterns of needs, requirements and aspirations. A *culture of diversity* is sensitive to difference and seeks to respond to groups in different ways.

Culture of uniformity	Culture of diversity
Same treatment for all.	Sensitive to difference.
Assumes all have similar needs and requirements.	Tailored provision.

s raises a number of troubling issues. Notions of equity and of universal entitlements to services were enshrined in the cultures of local authorities as they developed services in the post war era. They are being challenged from two different directions: firstly from groups themselves as black and ethnic minority groups, women, people with disabilities and other groups have sought services which are responsive to their requirements, and which are delivered in a non-discriminatory way. Secondly, universal access and entitlements have been challenged by financial restraints which increasingly require local authorities to target their services.

These two different pressures challenge the often bland 'equal opportunity' statements and require local authorities to deal with difficult issues. For example in the case of one of the leisure centres setting up user groups quoted in the previous section, it soon emerged that different groups wanted different things. A male 'black elders'' group, dominant on the management committee of the centre, wanted a meeting place open for long hours. An Asian girls' group wanted sessional activities, but could not come to the centre when the elders' group was there. Cultural barriers prevented them being adequately represented on the management committee. In attempting to be 'user driven' and 'community controlled', then, the leisure centre found that it could not adequately deal with issues of diversity.

The uniformity/diversity dimension also applies to the staff of a local authority, and to the political make-up of the council.

Uniformity	Diversity
Recruitment practices tend to mean the same type of person is usually appointed.	A wide diversity of staff are recruited to the organisation.
Everyone assumed to be equal.	Differences are valued.
Members tend to come from the same mould.	Members recruited from a wide range of different population groups.

The issue of member and staff diversity clearly impact on an authority's capacity to respond to the diversity of users and communities it serves.

Centralised/decentralised

Issues of decentralisation are usually considered in terms of structures and structural change. Here I want to consider cultural factors which may support or impede genuine change. A *strongly centralised* culture will retain large elements of power and control, both political and managerial, at the centre. There will be little devolution of real power to local offices, area committees, or business unit managers. A *strongly decentralised* culture will have genuine devolution of power. This may mean decentralisation of control for certain kinds of decision-making to area committees, and/or the devolution of responsibility to managers. The centre will develop a facilitating and enabling role in relation to both processes, and central departments and units will stress their role as service provider to the rest of the authority.

Centralised	Decentralised
Strong control by the centre.	Centre seen as having an enabling role
Little devolution of real power.	
Centre as regulator.	High levels of devolution.
	Centre as service provider.

However it is the *relationship* between centralisation and decentralisation which is important. Processes of decentralisation always involve two-way flows of power. Some powers are devolved, but at the same time the centre will develop new forms of power (for example setting standards, monitoring what happens and reviewing performance). There needs to be clarity about what kinds of powers are being devolved, what the limits to these powers are, and who is accountable to whom for what, in order to avoid 'mixed messages' about the extent of local freedoms and discretion. How this is done, and what happens when things go wrong (for example when a business unit or area committee makes a bad decision) is of critical importance. It is difficult to have real devolution without an element of trust, and cultures of trust are hard to build and notoriously easy to destroy.

Hierarchical/democratic

Many processes are challenging the hierarchical traditions of local government, from the 'flattening' of hierarchies through the cutting of tiers of middle management, through the use of new information technology which potentially broadens access to information and opens debate, to the emphasis on 'empowering' staff in order to deliver quality and flexibility in front line services. Old status divisions (size of offices, quality of desk, allocation of car park spaces, access to staff canteen and so on) are being eroded.

Hierarchical	Democratic
Respect for seniors expected.	Collegial.
Formal relationships.	Informal relationships.
Status divisions visible.	Status divisions weak.
Exclusions overt.	Exclusions covert.
Rewards through promotion.	Rewards in the work itself?

There is, however, an issue of who is included, and who excluded, in the new collegiality. Does it span all levels, or only the top tiers? Does it cross clerical, manual and professional grades? How might the informal and collegial processes serve to further exclude female or black members of staff from access to the real sources of power? What new forms of informal status divisions might be emerging? Finally, and perhaps most difficult, what patterns of reward and development are appropriate to an authority where opportunities for promotion have become a rarity as the old hierarchy has disappeared?

Reactive/proactive

The final dimension concerns a local authority's, department's or unit's strategic capacity. A *reactive culture* will tend to wait until events take place (whether this is a change of legislation or a financial crisis), and react to them afterwards. It will probably take an incremental view of policy, making small adjustments at the margins year on year. It will be more likely to make a lot of small changes as a response to a host of different pressures, rather than to develop an integrative approach. A proactive culture, in contrast, will attempt to take the initiative, and to influence its political environment (at the level of both local communities and national government, and even beyond to that of the EC). It will anticipate the future, and attempt to develop coherent and integrated strategies to meet future challenges.

Reactive	Proactive
Responds to pressures.	Takes initiative.
Reacts.	Seeks to influence.
Concerned with the present.	Anticipates the future.
Multiple initiatives.	Integrative and coordinated approach.

It is not that one is strategic and the other not, but that these draw on different models of strategy. The reactive culture may shape strategy out of emergent processes and responses within the organisation and the communities it serves, while the proactive culture will be able to articulate a clear sense of direction and to provide a vision of the future. Both approaches may be needed. The following chapter will develop this theme through a discussion of 'adaptive' and 'transformational' approaches to cultural change.

Using the cultural dimensions in culture mapping

The dimensions I have described can be used to suggest fruitful areas to explore through the techniques of cultural analysis (discussions, questionnaires and so on) outlined in Chapter 3. A further suggestion is that of 'plotting' your current culture on grids based on pairs of dimensions, and then identifying the desired direction of change (see Figure 4.2).

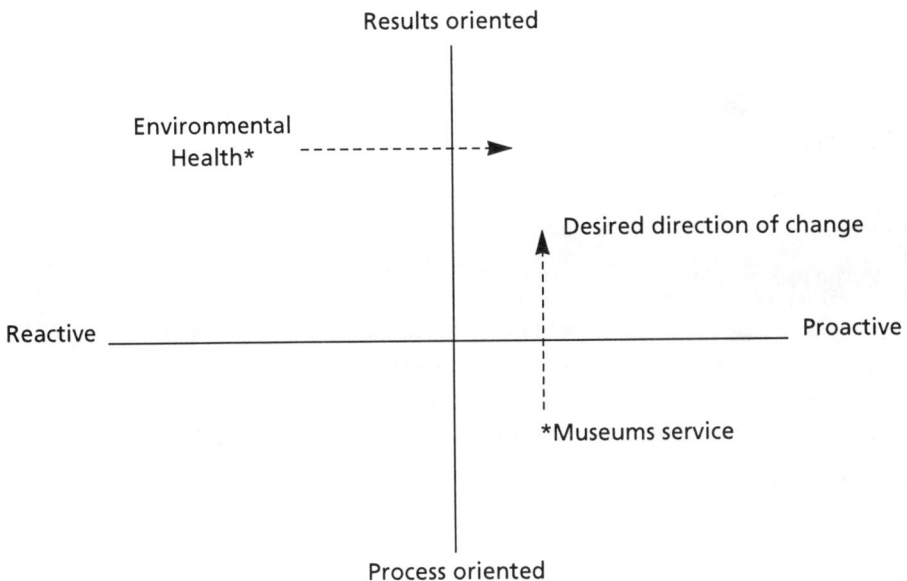

Figure 4.2

A planning team mapped its strengths and weaknesses as shown in Figure 4.3, adding the cultural dimension 'male/female' to highlight an issue of both staffing and style it wished to address.

It then identified its desired directions of change as shown in Figure 4.4 (see page 61).

Shaping organisational cultures in local government

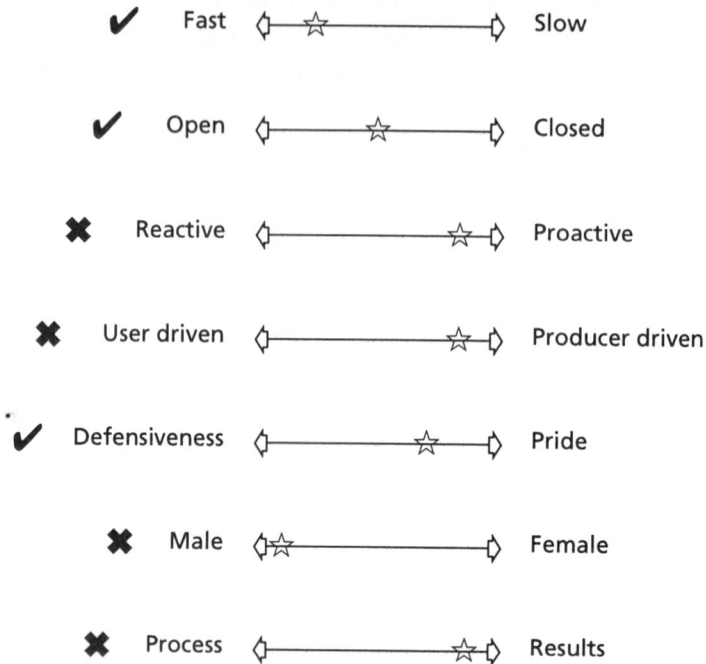

✔	Fast	◁—☆————▷	Slow
✔	Open	◁————☆———▷	Closed
✖	Reactive	◁————————☆▷	Proactive
✖	User driven	◁—————————☆▷	Producer driven
✔	Defensiveness	◁—————☆———▷	Pride
✖	Male	◁☆—————————▷	Female
✖	Process	◁—————————☆▷	Results

Figure 4.3

Mapping your culture

1 Select two dimensions which are of significance for your organisation, and draw a grid in which one dimension is represented by the horizontal axis, one by the vertical. For example, a social services provider unit might select the dimensions of managerial/professional and loose/tight.

2 Plot the current position of your organisation (or a part of your organisation).

3 Plot the 'ideal' position(s) in the light of your strategic goals.

4 What kind of changes are required?

5 Repeat for other pairs of dimensions.

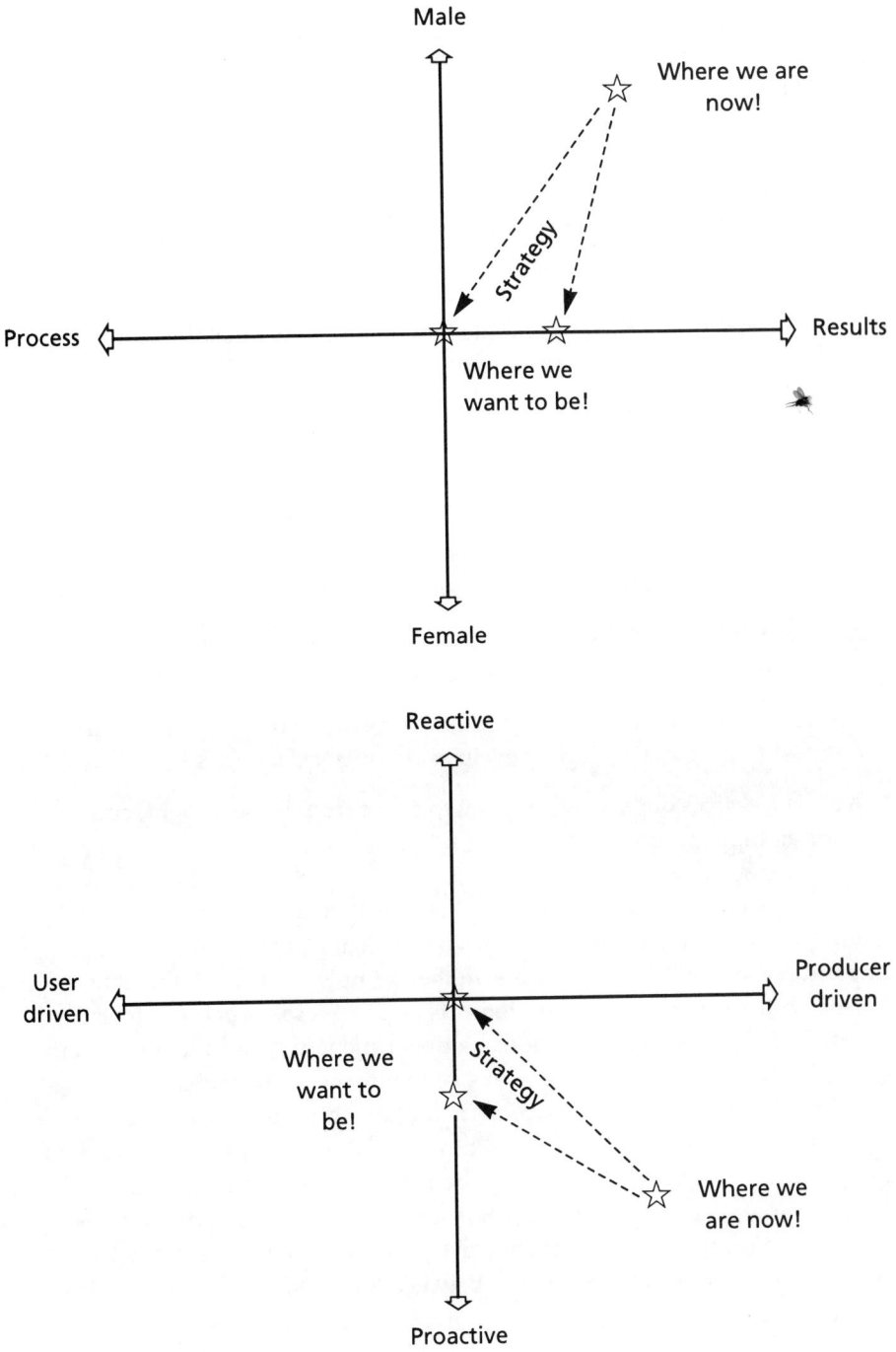

Figure 4.4

Questions for managers and members

- *What are the cultural dimensions that are most significant for our organisation/ department/unit?*

- *How would we assess our strengths and weaknesses on each of the dimensions we have selected?*

- *What are the significant areas of difference within the organisation in terms of the dimensions we have chosen as significant?*

Mapping your culture can suggest the kind of shifts that may be required to deal with new challenges and demands. Some typical results of using these cultural dimensions to plot desired change might include:

- A project team working at the centre recognising the need to move from hierarchical to democratic; and from closed to open.

- A finance division recognising the need to shift from process to results orientation; and from producer to user driven.

- A housing department exploring how to shift from uniformity to diversity.

- A personnel department facing CCT looking at the need to shift from moralist to pragmatist; and from closed to open boundaries.

- A social services department having to move from loose to tight, and wanting more pragmatism.

Mapping the culture, however, is likely to reveal the need not to replace one culture with a completely different one, but to change the balance between different sets of values and practices. In the examples just listed, the finance division will need to retain some elements of process focus in order to ensure probity and accountability. The housing department may need to retain some areas of uniformity to guarantee equity of treatment, while seeking to introduce more diversity of services to respond to different requirements and needs. The personnel department might well wish to retain some elements of 'moralism' as the guardian of equality policies; and the social services department will need to retain a process focus in areas of high risk such as child protection services. Overall, however, the cultural balance needs to change in each case, and the tensions between 'old' and 'emergent' cultures need to be carefully managed.

CHAPTER REVIEW

This chapter has argued that:

- Typologies of culture can help in identifying cultural strengths and weaknesses, and in mapping the different cultures which may exist (and the possible tensions between them).

- The most useful way of plotting a culture is through assessing it along a series of cultural dimensions, rather than as one of a series of 'types'.

- Ten dimensions relevant to local government are those of:

Process oriented	Results oriented
Moralist	Pragmatist
Open	Closed
Managerial	Professional
Loose	Tight
User/community driven	Producer driven
Uniformity valued	Diversity valued
Reactive	Proactive
Centralised	Decentralised
Hierarchical	Democratic

- The process of cultural mapping can help identify cultural strengths and weaknesses, and suggest where change may be needed.

- Change is rarely about moving from one type of culture to another, but is more concerned with balancing different cultural features.

5

Cultural change: developing the approach

THIS CHAPTER:

Aims to enable local authorities to develop an approach to change which is fitted to their goals. It:

- Sets out the characteristics of adaptive and transformational change.

- Explores a range of approaches to change which reflect different local authority characteristics and purpose.

- Looks at the interaction between structures and cultures in bringing about change.

- Includes a series of 'self-assessment' questions for local authority politicians and managers.

Managerial fashion often seems to suggest all-purpose solutions to change. Any recent textbook will provide a 'recipe' which will include ingredients such as decentralisation, devolution, flexibility, flat hierarchies, team based working and so on. What will emerge from any study of local authority change, however, is a variety of patterns which reflect different kinds of organisational purpose, as well as the unique cultures and traditions of each authority. The *purposes* and *processes* of change need, then, to reflect the characteristics of a specific local authority.

Adaptation or transformation? Identifying the need for change

The first part of developing an approach to change is to determine what kind of change is required, and when. Cultural change may be *adaptive* or *transformational*. Cultural adaptation is the least disruptive and, given a relatively stable environment, usually the most successful form of change. But it is slow, and cannot accommodate the radical change agendas which local authorities have faced in recent years. Typically, when first faced with new pressures and demands the response will tend to be incremental: that is, absorbing the external pressures within the existing organisational configuration and practices. If the pace of externally driven change is slow enough, this kind of change will produce an adaptive response in which the organisation will move slowly through a sequence of incremental steps. New solutions will 'emerge', new attitudes will develop over time and change will be successful because of the high levels of involvement of and participation by staff in developing new ways of working. Change will be absorbed with minimum disruption, and morale will tend to stay high. Figure 5.1 shows a process of successful adaptation, where external pressure is absorbed and internal capacity develops incrementally.

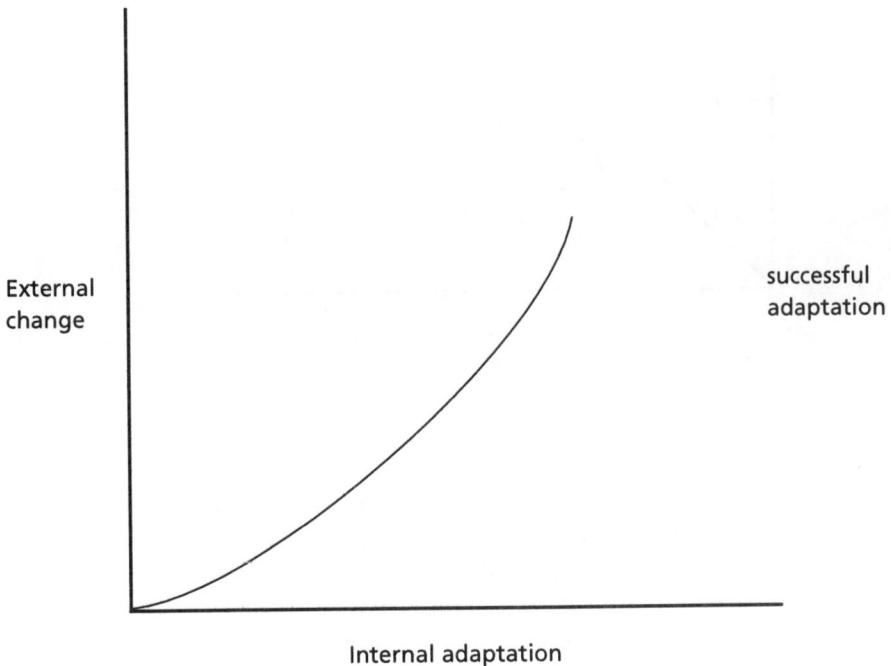

External change

successful adaptation

Internal adaptation

Figure 5.1

In the real world of local government through the 1980s and 1990s few, if any, local authorities have been able to accommodate change in this way. When the pace of external pressure builds up, the result places great strain on

65

existing structures, systems and cultures. This often results in a series of too many separate corporate change initiatives which appear incoherent to staff and users. Alternatively, the pressure on senior managers produces a series of crisis management responses. A typical change trajectory looks something like that depicted below (Figure 5.2) .

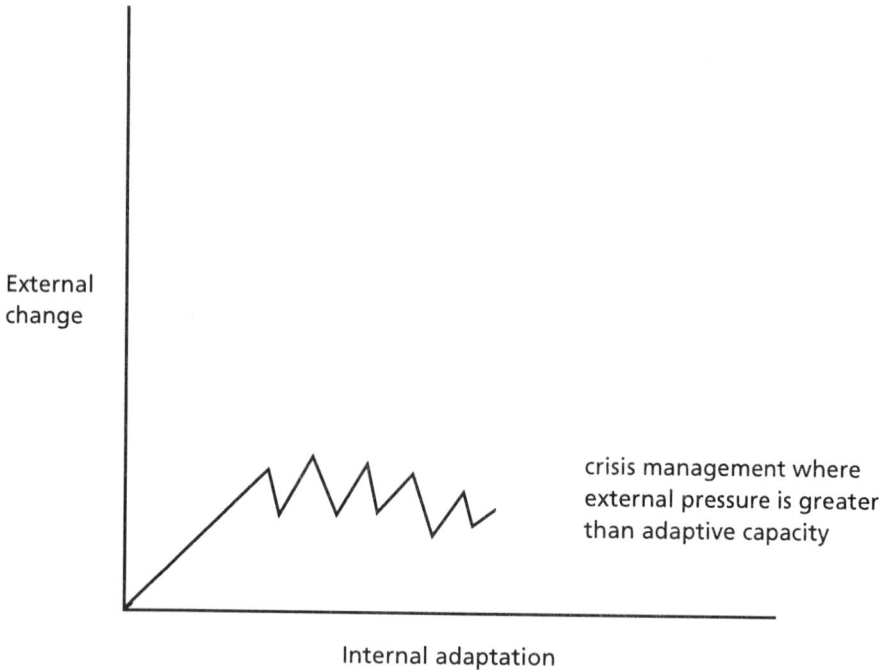

Figure 5.2

This shows a situation in which at relatively low levels of external pressure the organisation has been able to deal with change successfully through adaptation. As the pressure has built up, however, it has outstripped internal capacity, and has produced a series of crisis management, reactive responses. If continued these will further reduce internal capacity by lowering morale and undermining any sense of purpose and direction. What is required is a recognition of the point at which transformation, rather than adaptation, is called for. The purpose of such a transformation is to increase the internal capacity for change to a point at which it can successfully produce the results required today and have the capacity to absorb further changes in the foreseeable future. Figure 5.3 shows a shift from incremental to transformational change.

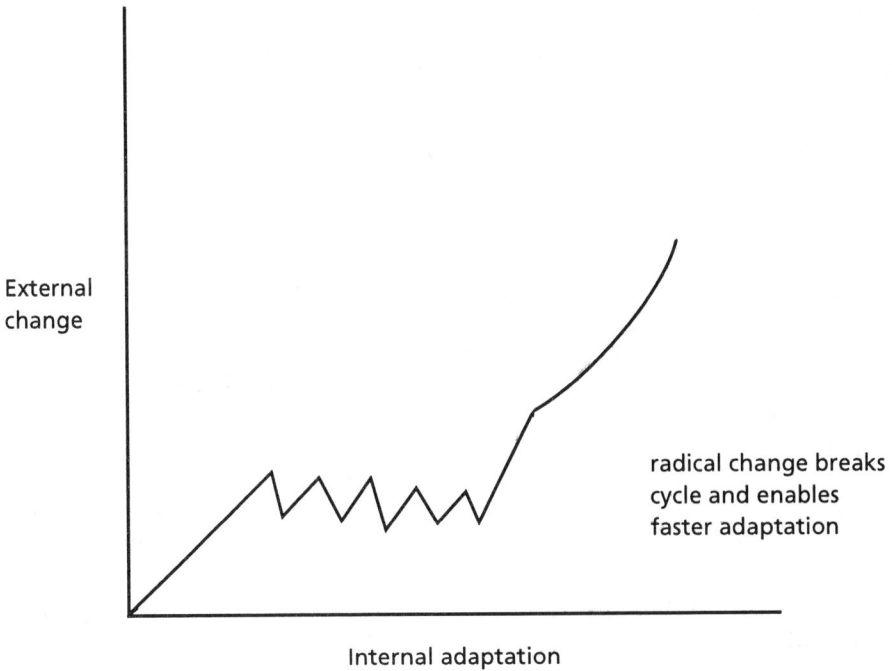

External
change

radical change breaks
cycle and enables
faster adaptation

Internal adaptation

Figure 5.3

Questions for managers and members

Question 1: How would you represent the process of change which your organisation has experienced on a similar graph?

Question 2: What are the pressures or demands which may lead to recognition of the need for more fundamental change in your local authority (or department/unit)?

Supporting the process of adaptation

Adaptation is in many ways the most appropriate model for cultural change. Attitudes and values, ways of working, behaviours and practices, relationships and all of the other core features of culture require a long time-frame to change. But adaptation does not take place 'naturally'. The model of culture outlined in Chapter 1 suggested that the view of organisations as organisms going through a natural process of evolution is flawed. Human intervention is required, and senior managers must create the conditions within which successful adaptation can occur. These include:

- A clear sense of direction.

- Leadership which provides a sense of purpose and coherence to the different changes required.

- The fostering of organisational synergies.

- Championing and supporting new ideas: creating a climate of innovation.

- Removal of barriers to change (e.g. over-hierarchical structures; over-formalised reporting procedures; even key individuals).

- The creation of opportunities for feedback and learning: both 'hard' (e.g. improved management information systems) and 'soft' (e.g. listening to staff and users; the use of action learning as a management development tool).

- A strategy process which enables the organisation to build on good practice and to shape strategy from incremental adaptations. This is what Mintzberg refers to as 'emergent strategy', in which strategy is seen as '. . . a pattern in a stream of decisions'. Senior management's role is to recognise and shape the pattern and feed it back to the organisation. One of the images Mintzberg uses for this is of the potter's wheel, in which strategy is 'crafted' by senior management from the organisational clay of incremental change (Mintzberg 1987, 1994).

- Personnel policies which support change through recruitment, development and communication.

Question 3: How well does your local authority support the process of adapting to external change?

Recognising the need for transformation

The organisational literature suggests that transformative change is usually triggered by some kind of crisis: the perception of a problem that cannot be resolved within existing frames of reference and organisational resources, and which requires some kind of fundamental organisational shift. For example Lundberg (1985) sets out a number of internal and external 'enabling conditions' within which cultural change is likely to take place, the 'precipitating pressures' which lead to a recognition of the need for change, and the 'triggering events' which stimulate the launch of change programmes.

Enabling conditions

Lundberg talks of the necessity for sufficient change resources, a strong leadership team, the capacity of systems to support change, and the existence of mechanisms through which change across a whole organisation can be integrated and coordinated. In local government this suggests that cultural change is only likely to 'take off' where there is clear commitment and leadership from both politicians and managers.

It is likely to be more successful where systems are capable of supporting it. For example attempts to devolve responsibility require responsive and user focused financial systems, and well developed management information systems. Local authority-wide change programmes are only likely to take off successfully where there are mechanisms to integrate the work of different departments.

Precipitating pressures

'Precipitating pressures' may include legislation; a resource crisis; new performance demands from communities, customers or members. They may also be the result of the demands placed on a local authority to work in new ways with partners in the private, public and voluntary sectors, or to respond to a more competitive environment.

Triggering events

The 'triggering event' may take the form of a change in political control; the appointment of a new chief executive (or, in the case of a department, a new director); a financial crisis; some kind of a major external stimulus to change (for example local government review) or internal failure (anything from negative public opinion on services to the results of an internal enquiry).

The Local Government Management Board study *Challenge and Change* (1993) described the conditions for achieving what they termed 'take off': the recognition of the need for, and initiation of, change. These were:

1 The importance of change agents at a senior level, notably the chief executive and political leadership.

2 The importance of the pressure of external change.

3 The importance of a key event which had a catalytic effect in transforming management philosophy.

The authors argued that:

> It is clear that external change is not enough to explain the development of new approaches to management. All authorities have been subject to the same set of external pressures, to a greater or lesser extent. Yet some responded by changing their management approaches in a radical way, while others have muddled through (Leach et al., LGMB 1993 p. 23).

The presence of change agents at a senior level was seen by the local authorities on which the study was based to have been a more significant force for change than the external pressures to which local authorities had been exposed. Typically the change agent had been a chief executive; sometimes a majority group leader and chief executive acting in partnership; more rarely a majority group leader alone. The study also showed that a positive political attitude pressing for change had not been necessary; '. . . response, support or acquiescence is enough' (Leach et al., LGMB 1993 p. 25).

These comments suggest the significance of leadership in shaping and communicating the organisation's response to change. In the public sector, however, change can rarely be driven through by one person alone; and in local authorities there is a need to build the commitment of management team and members by convincing them of the need for change.

Question 4: How far are the 'enabling conditions' for cultural change present in your local authority?

– What are the precipitating pressures and triggers for change?

– To what extent is the need for change recognised?

What kind of approaches to change is best suited to your local authority?

Each local authority's or department's culture and history will influence the ways in which it will approach the management of change. The dominant approaches to change can be characterised in terms of a number of dimensions:

Incrementalism/radicalism

This dimension reflects the 'adaptive' or 'transformational' approaches discussed in this chapter.

Integrative/fragmented

This dimension is concerned with how far change is designed to encompass the whole organisation or how far it is on a department by department basis.

Centralised/decentralised

This is concerned with how far initiatives are driven from the top or how far they are shaped from below. It reflects the extent to which power is devolved or decentralised (and the relative weight attached to 'bottom up' consultation and communication processes).

Open/closed

This dimension reflects how far decision-making processes are open to a diversity of voices and agendas, whether these stem from within the organisation or arise in local communities of interests. Open approaches are characterised by higher degrees of learning and adaptation as change unfolds.

Different local authorities have tended to manage change in different ways in response to the realignment of their purpose and role through the 1980s and 1990s. While each local authority is unique, it is possible to identify some common patterns of change management which tend to correspond with the different models of local authority purpose set out in the Local Government Management Board's *Fitness for Purpose* report (LGMB 1993).

> **Community governance:** *Those local authorities which have attempted to realign themselves in order to provide a strong lead on issues of concern to their local area (or region) have undertaken programmes of radical change. They have carried out wide ranging restructurings in order to realign departments and committees around new corporate and strategic priorities. Change has tended to be driven strongly from the centre. Although there has been a drive towards integration, a cultural gap between the centre and other parts of the organisation is not uncommon. This culture may be open or closed, although there is a tendency for closure once the corporate agendas have been determined. There is little room for further adaptation and learning once the momentum for change has been established.*

> **Business:** *Those local authorities which have adopted a 'business' or 'commercial' approach have seen radical change programmes accompanied by relatively extensive internal and external fragmentation. Change has generally been designed to give high levels of devolution and autonomy to business units. This has tended to result in a strong internal tension between top down and bottom up change. Resistance to corporate agendas and integrative mechanisms is often strong. Units may differ on the 'open/closed' dimension of change, depending on how far they take account of customer feedback. However there is a tendency towards closure because of the specification of tight performance requirements.*

Modified traditional: *This represents fairly traditional local authority structures with strong departmentalism but in which there have been efforts to change the culture to one which is more responsive to users and communities. There will be great variation in how far the cultures of different departments adopt open or closed and centralised or decentralised approaches to change. However across the local authority as a whole change is likely to be incremental rather than radical. Departments are likely to have high internal integration but to be very loosely integrated within the authority as a whole.*

Neighbourhood: *These local authorities are characterised by strong decentralisation and high levels of openness. However, integration at local level tends to be problematic if there is a strongly departmentalised culture at the centre. Similarly openness locally can lead to frustration (among both staff and community) in a culture with a strong centralist approach to change management.*

Question 5: How would you describe the typical approach to change within your local authority on each of the following dimensions of change management:

   Incremental - Radical

   Integrative - Fragmented

   Centralised - Decentralised

   Open - Closed

Local authority experience of change

Radical or incremental approaches

Many local authorities tended to adopt a gradualist approach which stresses the value of evolution and adaptation:

Development is through evolution, through continuous ways of working.

We use experiments to get change through; this is less threatening to vested interests and can be more challenging for those involved.

We have evolved rather than had a revolution.

An incremental approach can lead to good adjustment to change if it has a positive, rather than reactive, approach:

We have a willingness to implement change before the pain sets in.

It comes from being open; receiving information from as many sources as possible so that people can't be complacent about what they do.

We are prepared to challenge ourselves about whether we can improve.

Many that have successfully adopted such an approach in the past, however, have faced major challenges arising from the process of local government reorganisation. Major change cannot be accommodated within existing cultural frameworks, and radical reorganisation will inevitably be traumatic.

In contrast, other authorities have seen major structural change. Several illustrate how traumatic the process of radical change can be, sometimes leading to damaged relationships and a climate of mistrust. One Chief Executive commented that, with the benefit of hindsight, it was now recognised that a previous restructuring had been done in an unnecessarily brutal way:

> *The implications had not been discussed enough, and this created loads of angst and concern which set us back. Now we question whether it was really necessary.*

> *We realised that we hadn't consulted enough – staff knew we were looking to reduce numbers, rumour was rife, and morale hit rock bottom.*

This history meant that the introduction of changes tended to be treated with suspicion.

Continuity as well as change

The frequency of structural change is important. Service departments in particular tend to stress the need for consolidation as well as change on the basis that practitioner ownership requires a long term approach and staff stability and retention:

> *A culture that encourages managers and practitioners to move every few months will not ensure stability. Managers need to stay long enough to see through their mistakes and successes.*

Pace, as well as frequency, is significant:

> *Timing and pace is important – there is a need to sell an idea first to raise understanding, before specific details are outlined.*

> *Part of it is about the pace you move at. If you try to go too fast, you leave people behind. You need to go slowly enough to take 80 per cent with you, and train them for the new roles and skills.*

'Top down' or 'bottom up'

However it is not always possible to move slowly and take people with you as you go. One Director emphasised that different scenarios required different change strategies (see below), and commented:

> It is important to think about and be clear about what kind of change scenario we are in; and explore the implications for staff. It is vital that the implications for staff are not minimised or brushed aside. We don't necessarily succeed in this; we often think of personnel issues after, rather than before, the event.

CHANGE SCENARIOS

Legislation and other changes which have to be enacted fast.

Here the reasons for change are usually clear. The strategy is to inform people fast, and to explain the way in which the change is to be handled.

Internal reorganisations or service changes, perhaps stemming from senior managers or members.

Here there is room for flexibility, so the task is to seek views and elicit feedback from staff. The reasons for change may be unclear to staff and the emphasis should be on discussion *with* staff rather than just providing them with information.

Areas where the present system or structure is creaking at the seams, but there is no particular solution in mind.

The task here is to consult much more widely, set up a group to look at the problem, and seek feedback on proposed solutions. The focus here is on involvement, so that the reasons for change become evident to staff themselves.

The importance of internal communication is stressed repeatedly by managers who have led major changes:

> Don't assume that time spent talking to people is a waste of time. You will inevitably pay for it later if you don't.

> The link of staff communication has to be continual, not just something which happens at the start and end of a change cycle.

However, communication is not always straightforward. Choices have to be made about where to consult with staff before members, and where to talk to members first. Decisions may also be needed on whether to involve Trades Unions before or after talking to staff.

Overall a top down and bottom up approach which endeavours to develop and involve individuals, but at the same time to provide clear leadership and direction, is the most likely key to successful change.

Cultures and structures

Restructuring alone cannot bring about cultural change, and over-frequent restructurings tend to reduce the overall 'cultural capital' of an organisation – its internal and external networks, synergies between different forms of work, 'common sense' understandings of the channels through which things can get done, organisational skills, and ultimately morale and direction. As a result its overall capacity to deal with further change is reduced.

Nevertheless structural changes are usually required as part of a cultural change programme, for one or more of the reasons below.

Reasons for restructuring as part of a cultural change programme

- to bypass parts of the existing structure which are likely to resist change (however, this may be avoiding rather than confronting a problem);

- to send signals about the aim, focus and direction of change;

- to foster new kinds of working practices and working relationships;

- to realign departments to create synergies on strategic issues central to the corporate agenda (e.g. environmental issues);

- to devolve financial and other responsibilities;

- to decentralise in order to enhance responsiveness to local agendas and to integrate services to local communities;

- to separate commissioning and providing functions.

Recent restructurings have been led by a range of overt or covert agendas, from cost reduction to the removal of an established power base, which cross-cut the kinds of principles set out above. Where restructurings have been done on an *ad hoc* basis, however, the results have often been messy, leading to the need for yet another restructuring in a year or two years' time. One of the lessons to emerge in recent years is that many local authorities have perhaps spent undue amounts of energy on internal issues – planning, delivering, and solving the problems which arise from constant restructuring – and not enough on developing effective strategic responses to external change. Similarly, many have caused a great deal of *cultural destruction* – the loss of existing value present in established working relationships – through too many restructurings in too short a time.

Structures and cultures interact in complex ways. Any given structure will foster particular sets of working relationships and arrangements, and will make others difficult. For example strongly hierarchical structures tend to discourage horizontal ways of working. Strongly centralist, top down structures are likely to minimise openness and responsiveness to local communities and users. High levels of devolution or decentralisation can act as a barrier to common values and culture.

Structural and cultural changes also interact. It is difficult to sell a new 'vision' or direction of change when staff are insecure and uncertain about the next restructuring. Any cultural change programme will need to address potential barriers in existing structures. The key issue is whether such restructurings are visibly linked to some overall organisational purpose. A realignment of structures which is evidently informed by a positive set of values will help to develop new cultural orientations much more than a restructuring which is evidently geared towards cost reduction alone.

CASE STUDY

Change in a social services department

Social Services Department X had attempted to build and integrate a progressive culture through TQM (Total Quality Management). Its approach to change, however, had been adaptive rather than transformational, and change had not been fast enough to cope with new performance demands. It faced the following issues:

- provider units not able to compete in the marketplace, so purchasers facing cost stringencies were tending to select external providers;
- purchasers were not tackling the need to ration services;
- planners tended to have a short term perspective, seeing their task as that of producing the next community care plan rather than to engage with how it might be delivered through a managed market;

- the SMT (Senior Management Team) tended to be hands-on, task driven;
- there was a political reluctance to acknowledge areas of poor performance.

The approach to change required a double, interlocking agenda of soft (culture building) approaches together with hard (culture changing) levers. That is, it required:

At a departmental level:

- Positive leadership and a commitment by both political and managerial leaders to address the key issues through a strategic approach; *and*
- The setting of objectives and monitoring and review of performance.

At a divisional level:

- Support for new ways of working through training and development; *and*
- The requirement for each section to develop business plans with milestones and targets for change.
- The introduction of stronger quality assurance processes within the overall TQM framework.

Fundamentally what was required was the development of different divisional cultures with their own clear identity and rationale. This meant confronting differences of role and purpose – for example their different stakes in the quality agenda – as well as their common stake in the department as a whole. Restructuring had taken place several years ago. But cultural change had lagged behind.

Aligning structures, procedures and values

A simple mapping technique can be used to compare the cultural values one is seeking to establish with those underpinning and reinforced by existing structures, systems and procedures (see Figure 5.4). Desired cultural values are listed along the horizontal axis. Various aspects of the organisation's current structures, systems and procedures are noted on the vertical axis. Where these support the desired cultural values the intersection point shows a positive symbol; where they undermine them the intersection point shows a negative symbol.

Delivery mechanisms \ Values	Innovation	Openness	Business awareness	Teamwork	Cost containment	Flexibility
Leadership		✕	⊕			
Management style	✕				⊕	✕
Communications	⊕		⊕	⊕		
Resourcing		✕		⊕		
Development and training		⊕			⊕	
Rewards and recognition	⊕	✕	⊕		✕	
Systems/policies/procedures	✕					
Organisational structure		✕	✕			

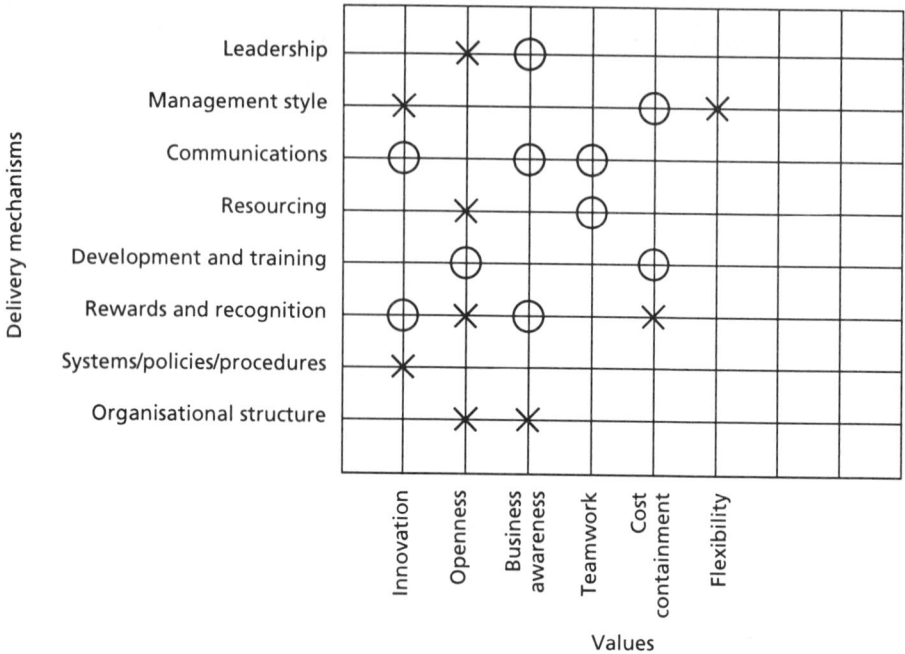

Figure 5.4   Culture mapping
Source: Storey and Sissons 1993 p. 192

The example from Storey and Sissons evaluates how far key organisational features support or undermine the cultural values of innovation, openness, business awareness, teamwork, cost containment and flexibility. The chart shows, for example, that the current style of leadership supports business awareness but not openness. While several of the new values are supported by the communication system, none are enhanced by the structure. Indeed, the structure actually militates against change.

The value of this tool is that, as Storey and Sissons argue, it draws attention to the fact that managing cultural change is not just a matter of trying to change attitudes and motivation. It is concerned with the realities of organisational structures, systems and practices which structure everyday experience.

CHAPTER REVIEW

This chapter has discussed different approaches to cultural change. It has argued that:

- Adaptive approaches are appropriate where external or political pressures for change are small enough to be accommodated incrementally.

- Transformational approaches are needed where a fundamental shift or realignment is required.

- Transformational programmes are most likely to succeed in the presence of enabling conditions and precipitating pressures as well as a key 'triggering event' which brings recognition of the need for change.

- Change programmes may differ in terms of incrementalism/radicalism, integration/fragmentation, centralisation/decentralisation, and in terms of degrees of openness and participation.

- Structural and cultural change need to be aligned, and to be supported by changes in systems and procedures.

6

Beyond the vision: developing a programme of change

THIS CHAPTER:

- Develops a framework for introducing cultural change.

- Explores issues of culture and power.

- Suggests how 'vicious circles' can be unlocked.

- Provides case studies of cultural change.

While there have been some notable successes, the public and private sectors are littered with the evidence of failures in achieving cultural change. There are three main reasons for such failures.

- The first is overexcitement on the part of senior managers, with too much hype and not enough substance, leading to cynicism on the part of staff.

- The second, in contrast, lies in lack of commitment and poor leadership on the part of senior managers (and in local government insufficient backing by members). As a result not enough resources or support are provided. Six months on, political priorities may have changed, or a key player has moved on and there is not enough momentum to sustain the initiative.

- The third lies in organisational attempts to 'engineer' cultural change through the mechanistic tools of structures and systems, plans and objectives. This is especially prevalent in the context of the bureaucratic and hierarchical traditions of local government, in which restructuring has often been used as the prime 'lever' of change, and in which top down controls have been the traditional means of implementing change.

Cultural change requires something more. There are three important requirements for any initiative:

1 It must have clear, positive and committed leadership.

2 The programme must be integrative – it must pull together, inform and integrate all change initiatives, so that change appears coherent; so that it provides a strong sense of direction and meaning for staff; and so that 'mixed messages' arising from conflicting goals of different change plans can be avoided.

3 The change programme must address the different 'layers' of an organisation through which culture is sustained – its symbols, practices and values.

A model of cultural change

Chapter 3 set out a framework for culture analysis based on three 'layers' of culture:

Symbols

(signals about what is important and valued in this organisation)

High profile symbols include:

- Buildings, layout and decor.
- Publicity and communication materials.
- Official language, especially visions, missions and statements.
- Ceremonies and traditions.
- Public style and corporate imagery (logos, uniforms etc.).
- Heroes and leaders.

Low profile symbols include:

- Language.
- Stories and jokes.
- Dress and appearance of staff.
- How people 'customise' the physical environment.
- Unofficial ceremonies and traditions.

Practices

(behaviour and action; 'how we do things around here')

- Routines.
- Patterns of interaction.
- Customs and norms of behaviour.
- Recipes for problem-solving and decision-making.
- How people use their time.
- Use of technology.

These are influenced and sanctioned by:

- Structures.
- Systems.
- Patterns of management coordination and control.
- Performance management systems.

Values

(deep structures of attitudes and beliefs)

Espoused values: those which the local authority officially strives for.
Embedded values: the deeply held values of staff, managers and members.

- Personal beliefs.
- Professional or occupational values.
- Attitudes towards the world and to others.
- Political and community allegiances.
- Values (e.g. 'public service' values).

Using the model

There are two important points about this 'layered' model of culture.

- The first is that as you move down the layers it is harder to intervene. It is relatively easy to manufacture new corporate symbols – mission statements, ceremonies, logos, publicity materials, decor and the like. It is much more difficult to change how people actually behave, and enormously difficult to change their beliefs and values.

- The second point is that for any cultural change to take place, *interventions are required at all three levels* ... The three-layer model of culture stresses the need to manage the 'hard' aspects of organisational processes – the systems, structures, practices – as well as the 'soft' elements of symbols, style and values.

New practices can be established through setting goals and targets, by rewarding new behaviour, by changing the support systems, and by monitoring and evaluating achievements. Particular values can be developed through training and through the identification and communication of statements of core values. The 'soft' aspects of change usually associated with culture – changes in values, style, relationships and informal norms and practices – need to be supported through changes in systems and procedures; through organisational structures; through performance management; through recruitment practices and reward systems, and through clear strategies and consistent decision making.

CASE STUDY

Equal opportunities

To illustrate the way in which intervention at different levels can be brought together in an overall programme of change we can use the example of 'equal opportunities'. Many equality initiatives can be seen as dealing with the level of symbols alone. The authority may produce a policy statement, change job advertisements to include an equalities slogan (e.g. 'we are working towards equal opportunities'), and ensure that 'correct' language is used in official communications. However unless this is linked to action it will only carry symbolic value.

Some authorities, in contrast, focus their intervention at the level of 'values' through programmes of equalities training designed to change attitudes. But unless new values are clearly supported by changes in practices they are unlikely to lead to real change.

One authority developed a three-level strategy as follows:

Changing the symbols

- New policy statement.
- Wording of job adverts.
- Appointment of new director on otherwise all white male senior management group.
- Use of non-discriminatory language.
- Chief executive statement on unacceptability of racial and sexual harassment.

Changing the practices

- Policy statement linked to performance targets.
- Positive recruitment strategies – e.g. use of minority press.
- Positive action training for women and black and ethnic minorities in professions or occupations in which they are under-represented.
- Changing the way the senior management team meetings work.
- Grievance procedures on issues of discrimination and harassment taken seriously and staff supported in using them.

Changing the values

- Clear statement of values.
- Equality values integrated into all training programmes.
- Training on equality issues linked to action learning.

Changing the symbols

New symbols may be created by the use of new language, communication of a new mission or vision, opening of a new building or redecoration of an existing one, key appointments and promotions, and so on. Low profile symbols within management control – their own actions, attention to particular kinds of detail, their use of time, the stories they tell, their physical presence or absence and other aspects of their practice which are likely to be scrutinised and interpreted by staff – can also be changed in an effort to send out new signals about what is important.

But it is not possible to change an organisation's values and beliefs, or its typical ways of 'doing things', by changing its symbols alone. What matters is how the symbols are interpreted: how people make meanings by drawing on the symbolic world they occupy. A glossy brochure can induce a sense of organisational pride in some contexts; in others it can induce cynicism. The way it is likely to be interpreted depends on the perceived gap between the symbol and the member of staff's perception of the organisational reality. This in turn is influenced by the way in which the meaning of the symbols is interpreted to them through both the statements and actions of senior managers, and by the level of involvement which people have had in constructing the symbols. It is important to remember that 'unofficial' interpretations of any new symbols will be carried through low profile symbols (jokes, gossip, stories) and that these lie outside the direct control of senior managers.

Changing the symbols involves:

1 Deciding what signals you want to send to organisation members, and to customers and stakeholders, about what is important and valued in this organisation.

2 Looking at existing symbols and exploring what signals they send.

3 Identifying what changes are needed to existing symbols, and where new symbols might need to be created.

4 Where new symbols are to be created, deciding how to involve staff in the process, and how to communicate the results.

Review question: what symbols do you think would signify each of the following core values?

– *Efficiency and cost consciousness.*

– *Caring for customers.*

– *Go-ahead and business oriented.*

– *Concerned for the environment.*

– *Community empowerment.*

What risks does each of them carry of creating a 'credibility gap'?

Encouraging new behaviours and practices

Local authorities can do a great deal to establish new behaviours by setting goals and targets, rewarding new behaviours, and by monitoring and evaluating achievements. They can also create the conditions which make change possible by, for example, eradicating outdated control systems which tie energy up in the wrong things, and by ensuring that financial and information systems support new practices. For example a move towards greater devolution and more 'proactive' management will only be effective if the organisational systems which support it are fast, flexible and user oriented.

Behaviours and practices are also shaped by organisational structures. For example, 'everyday patterns of interaction' are shaped by formal roles which set out who is supposed to relate to whom and in what ways (as manager to staff, as colleague to colleague, as support staff to front line staff and so on). Structures set out the framework in which relations are formed, but they do not determine them. Formal relationships are underpinned (or undermined) by informal cultures and patterns of interaction. As many local authorities have found, it is very difficult to do away with traditional bureaucratic patterns of relationship simply by 'flattening' the hierarchy or putting staff into teams. Old patterns of control cross-cut and undermine the new dotted lines and arrows on organisation charts.

In a similar way, 'formal' systems and 'informal' routines interact. New financial systems, information management systems, performance review systems, can create the conditions for new patterns of work. They also send important signals about the values and priorities of senior management. But on their own they do not 'unglue' old ways of doing things. For example E-mail may create the conditions in which sending memos becomes a thing of the past, but introducing E-mail does not on its own make bureaucratic routines wither away.

Changing behaviours, then, may involve:

1 Changing formal relationships and patterns of interaction through structural change.

2 Supporting new practices through organisational systems.

3 Embedding desired behaviours in appraisal and performance management systems.

4 Reflecting desired behaviours in the setting of goals and targets.

5 Rewarding new behaviours through formal (pay, promotion) and informal (praise) reward systems.

6 Training staff in new practices and the skills on which they are based.

Review question: what practices do you think would signify one or more of the following core values?

— *Efficiency and cost consciousness.*

— *Caring for customers.*

— *Go-ahead and business oriented.*

— *Concerned for the environment.*

— *Community empowerment.*

CASE STUDY

Quality and the poverty of rhetoric

Quality initiatives often get stuck at the symbolic level: that is, they may be characterised by a great deal of talk but not a lot of real changes in practice. The layered model of culture can be used to suggest different sites of action and involvement. Clear leadership is vital both in terms of symbols (leading the organisation into new sets of goals and values) and through actions (leaders practising the new values in their own style and behaviour). New systems need to be put in place, and new behaviours built into reward and appraisal processes. Performance management and review processes are needed to manage and monitor the new behaviours.

New, customer oriented values must be embedded through training. But real change will not come about simply by training front line staff in customer care. This is not an argument against such training. It is undoubtedly preferable, from the user's point of view, to deal with friendly and helpful staff. However the power of front line staff to respond to user needs and preferences is probably a more significant dimension of user satisfaction. This requires two important change issues to be considered.

The first is concerned with decisions about how far 'customer first' initiatives involve some change to existing power relationships. This refers to the devolution of power to front line staff to make decisions, and the power of customers or users to influence the shape and pattern of the services they receive. The second is about the clarity of the strategy. 'Customer first' initiatives raise a series of questions which must be addressed: *Who* is the

87

customer of a particular service? *How* are decisions about the needs or demands of diverse customers to be made? *How* are services to be rationed? *How* can disadvantaged users be supported in articulating their needs or wishes? *How* can the claims of current users and the needs of non users be balanced? *How far* can the perspectives of users be included in decisions about the design or delivery of services? *How* can the requirements of other stakeholders be balanced against the needs and views of consumers? The response to these questions determines what kind of cultural change an organisation is engaged in. Only when they are addressed will values be clear and change begin to be pervasive rather than cosmetic.

Espousing new values

Values, attitudes and beliefs are very significant in a public service context. People may have joined your local authority or one of its professions because of the values which are seen to underpin it, and that value base is one of the most potent mobilisers of energy and motivators of action.

Values are very difficult to change once adulthood is reached. They are influenced by a range of factors beyond the organisation's control. However, organisations can support change by providing new opportunities and experiences, including:

New information

Our knowledge about the world is one important source of our values and beliefs. However, it is perfectly possible to believe 'new' information at a cognitive level while holding on to core beliefs at an affective level. For example it is possible to hold 'traditional values' about order and control while understanding perfectly the environmental changes which have led to the need for more flexibility and openness. Communicating information can therefore only ever be a partial strategy. It needs to be linked to the requirement and expectation that such information will be translated into new practices. Nevertheless the power of providing fast feedback on such issues as user responses to services can be an important influence on behaviour.

New experience

This is rather more powerful than new information. Changing jobs, 'acting up', taking on new responsibilities, being 'seconded' to another department or another organisation, developing partnerships, are all potentially important levers of change. These kinds of opportunity can be managed. However, there is no guarantee of exactly what the resultant change will be. New experience needs to be linked to some opportunity to reflect and make sense of it. Mentoring, coaching, action learning and training can be used to support and reinforce the process of personal change and transition.

New peers

Other people – especially those in our primary reference groups – are an important source of validation and reinforcement of our values and beliefs. Joining a new team, becoming involved in a new group project, taking up a new social activity, or becoming part of a group undergoing a common experience (e.g. members of a training programme), all are important sources of value reinforcement or possible value shift.

New powers

Real power to influence decisions can change attitudes by inducing a stronger sense of involvement and identification. If the current rhetoric of 'staff empowerment' is realised this will, then, be a major source of cultural change. More modest attempts to devolve power – for example financial and personnel powers – to business managers can also lead to significant attitude changes. Whether these are the right changes is another question.

New motivators

One of the most evident forms of this in the recent past has been exposure to competition. The most significant example is probably the culture changes which have occurred rapidly in most departments or units which have been subject to CCT. Other powerful new motivators lie in the sharpening of competition for jobs, the introduction of fixed term employment contracts, and new reward systems such as PRP (Performance Related Pay). Many of these are, however, negative rather than positive motivators. They invoke individual or sectional interests rather than a strong sense of values.

New models

This refers to the kind of leadership which people are exposed to and influenced by. Exposure to positive models can be very influential in shaping individual beliefs and responses, but only where staff are able to identify in some way with the model. This has significant implications for women and for black and ethnic minority staff who often have few positive leadership models with whom they can identify.

Missions, visions and values

At the heart of any cultural change initiative lies a redefinition of values or purpose. This can take the form of one or more of the following:

- A statement of the *values* which a local authority or department wishes to see represented in the way in which it goes about its work.
- A statement of the *mission or purpose* of the authority or department.
- A statement of the *core goals* which it wishes to pursue.

The purpose of such statements is primarily *affective* ... They provide a vision of the future which gives meaning to change, gives staff a sense of purpose, and provides a symbolic representation of change which is simple enough for staff to understand, remember and use. Its primary focus is internal rather than external. While such statements may be used to send signals to stakeholders and customers, they must be much more than a PR exercise. They must be understood and 'lived' at all levels of the organisation.

Statements of values and purpose tell the organisation what it is for, and what is expected of those who work for it. They help people decide what is important and give a sense of purpose and direction. They should be:

- Simple enough to understand.
- Clear enough to be communicated.
- Inspirational enough to provide a sense of meaning and purpose.
- Focused enough to guide difficult decisions.
- Explicitly related to the processes of deciding priorities, setting objectives and determining plans.

Communicating the values

Statements of mission and values are actively interpreted not passively consumed. People make meanings by drawing on the symbolic world they occupy, but meanings are constructed through social processes and cannot directly be implanted from above. The way such statements are likely to be interpreted depends on:

- The level of involvement which people have had in constructing or actively discussing their production.

Care must be taken about how this is done so as to avoid a result which is meaningless or vacuous. Complete consensus or 'design by committee' is not the ultimate goal. But the costs of wide discussion before the production of any such statement will be more than repaid in the knowledge and even 'ownership' of it afterwards. Some local authorities have used the introduction of 'Investors in People' to stimulate such discussions.

- The way in which the symbols are communicated and interpreted to staff.

Most local authorities who have produced a statement of core goals and values have recognised the importance of communication, and many have produced posters, leaflets, cards and so on. The problem is that these are predominantly a passive rather than active channel of communication. Staff should be given the chance to discuss the content of the message so that they can explore what it means in the context of their own work, and their knowledge and understanding should be reviewed from time to time.

- The perceived gap between symbols and staff's perception of the 'real world', especially as expressed in the actions of senior management.

Meaning is derived as much from 'low profile symbols' – language, stories, jokes and so on – as from the high profile, 'official' missions and visions. Unfortunately (from the point of view of senior managers) it is managerial actions that are perhaps the most prolific source of gossip and stories, and their decisions, actions, and informal comments will be closely scrutinised to identify the real intent behind any change initiative. Any action which is inconsistent with the newly espoused philosophy is likely to seriously undermine it.

It is unrealistic to attempt to change a culture by changing the values of all those within it so that there is some kind of eventual whole-organisation 'consensus' around a new set of values. Rather, it is necessary to think of values as something which different groups within an organisation will mobilise as the struggles which accompany change are played out, and the tensions which change produces are resolved. Value change is rarely about changing the values of an entire organisation. It is more usually about a change in the balance of power between members and officers promoting different sets of values.

Reinforcing new values through HRM practices

Changing values, beliefs and attitudes often means changing people, especially those in key positions. Recruitement, selection and, in many cases, the way in which redundancy is organised are then an integral part of any cultural change strategy.

- A change in leadership can bring new ideas into the organisation, and if coupled with a strong power base, can be a major impetus to cultural change.

- Internal promotion and reward policies also need to be reviewed. Changing the type of person deemed suitable for advancement (whether this means promotion, selection for a key project team, secondment to the corporate centre or selection for a high profile training programme) is a necessary, but often neglected, component of cultural change. This means that person specifications, and assumptions about what kind of person should be chosen for other forms of advancement, need to be carefully scrutinised.

- The reorganisation (and sometimes relocation) of staff into new configurations and groups can be important in unlocking old constraints and barriers to change, or in introducing a more participative style of management. Quality circles and project teams are obvious examples.

- Management education and development is an integral element of any HRM strategy. Management development can help bring about cultural change, especially where it links training opportunities to workplace practice through action learning and work related projects.

- Cultural change is concerned with opening the organisation up to new ideas and with recognising the contribution of the whole, rather than some of, its workforce. An organisation which values diversity and which draws on the skills, talents, ideas and perspectives (including critical perspectives) of different kinds of people within its workforce will be much better placed to sustain real change than one which can only recognise and hear the voices of a few.

Culture and power

Managing cultural change means confronting the barriers. These include vested interests who wish to defend established power bases. But resistance

92

may also arise from those who wish to hold on to existing values and t defend the organisation against changes which they see as against the interests of users, communities or staff as a whole. While 'vested interests may need to be challenged and their power base reduced, 'value defenders' represent something rather different. Rather than seeking to 'overcome' resistance, it is often useful to reconceptualise 'resisters' in terms of 'defenders' and to ask, for each resisting force or group, 'What is being defended?' Resistance may be grounded in a fear of the loss of something that was central to past culture and which is seen as having value for the future (for example the public service values which many see as being displaced by managerial or market imperatives).

Culture is a site in which competition between different and conflicting values is played out (e.g. between the values of professionalism and managerialism or between efficiency and equity). It is the site of conflict over meanings (e.g. over whether new initiatives are to be seen as unblocking old constraints, or as presenting new threats). It is the site in which power bases are shifted and realigned as groups are mobilised to support or resist change. Individuals may learn the rhetoric of new values and adopt new cultural symbols in order to defend or expand their power base. It is also the site in which definitions of 'insiders' (guardians of the culture) and 'outsiders' (those who challenge traditional meanings and values) are realigned.

These processes operate within both member and officer groups, and complex alliances may form across political, managerial and community interests. Cultural change, then, requires political skills in both senses of the word: the excercise of political skills by councillors, and the management of organisational politics. In both cases, unlocking what holds the past in place is as important as inspiring all with a new future. That is why an understanding of 'vicious circles' are important.

Unlocking vicious circles

Culture tends to reproduce itself over time. Practices become deeply embedded, and self-replicating 'vicious circles' become established. To unlock vicious circles it is necessary to refocus, moving from thinking in terms of desired future states (what do we need to create) to thinking about continuities (what keeps things the same; what cultural imperatives keep traditional patterns of behaviour and beliefs in place).

Begin with a practice which you think acts as a barrier to change. The problem needs to be defined in terms of behaviour (e.g. 'we tend to be too ready to blame each other or look for scapegoats when things go wrong'). The next step is to 'brainstorm' ways in which this practice is sustained. Begin by listing all of the relevant factors that anyone in the group can think of. Write them up and then try to explore relationships between them by drawing arrows which connect key things together. Represent what you see as causal or influencing relationships by arrows indicating the direction of the flow. It may be that you end up being able to draw a 'vicious circle' which connects a number of these together (see Figure 6.1).

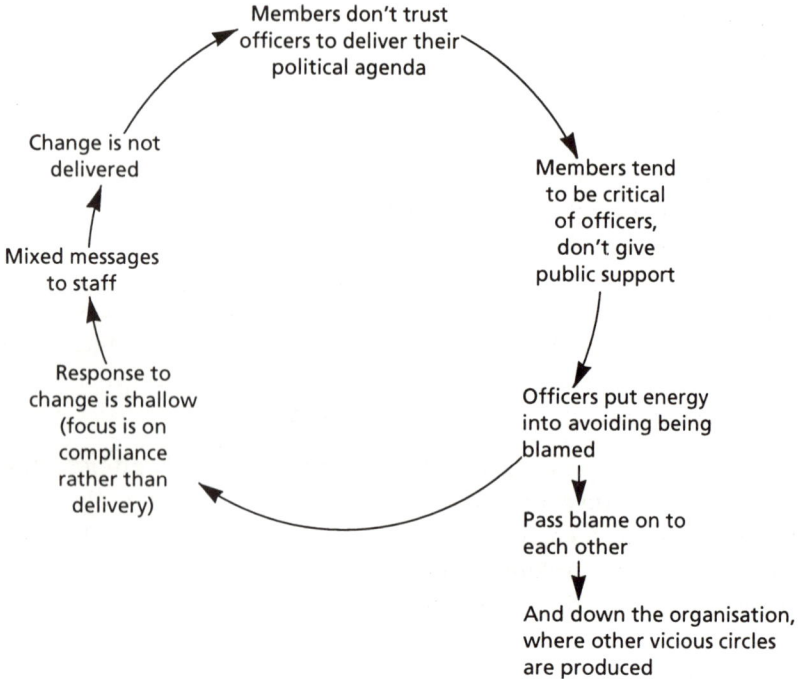

Figure 6.1   The 'vicious circle' of a blame culture

The task is then to look at how you might be able to intervene to break the cycle of events. For change to be effective it is usually necessary to break the cycle at several different points, producing a range of responses to the problem:

- more joint discussions and workshops with members and officers about how change can be delivered

- leader/lead group tell members that public blaming of officers is not acceptable

- Chief Executive sends messages about conduct of senior management group and backs this by not allowing/sanctioning internal blame and competitive behaviour

- real attempts to develop a learning culture at officer and member levels

- work to change attitudes of senior managers, and replace some

- advertise successes and reward new behaviour at all levels

- ensure the mechanisms are in place to deliver the long term changes members seek

- develop a learning approach to performance management and review

If you wish to explore these ideas further, you may wish to look at Charles Hampden-Turner's *Corporate culture: from vicious to virtuous circles* (1990), or Edward do Bono's *Water Logic* (1993).

The 'vicious circles' technique illustrates some important features of dealing with issues of culture. We are dealing with deeply embedded beliefs and behaviour which are not amenable to change through conventional rational planning techniques. A more organic understanding of change is required:

Rational planning approaches	Organic approaches
Goal oriented.	Process oriented.
Linear.	Patterns of interconnection.
Top down.	Pervasive.
Focus on change.	Focus on continuity (what keeps things the same).

This organic model directs attention to understanding how the current situation is reproduced. It turns change on its head, focusing on understanding what exists now rather than what ought to be. This is a very necessary part of the analysis, requiring sensing and understanding rather than planning and goal setting. It leads to the kinds of change strategy which are about shaping, moulding and crafting change rather than starting afresh with a blank sheet of paper. However it has one significant limitation. It tends to ignore issues of power. To overcome barriers to change and to unblock old ways of doing things requires changes in the ways in which resources are allocated, changes in who gets recruited and promoted, and changes in organisational structures.

Cultural change in practice

Many of the themes of this chapter can be illustrated through a case study of culture and change at Wrekin District Council, one of the earliest and most ambitious programmes of cultural change in a local authority context.

CASE STUDY

Culture change at Wrekin District Council

A study of the development of the distinctive culture at Wrekin D.C. (McLean and Marshall, 1988) highlighted the following factors as having been significant forces for development and change:

1 Importing difference into the authority: people, ideas and methods.

2 Restructuring: the most important aspect of which was that it signalled the need for change. By itself, it would have done little to change the culture.

3 Championing leadership from the chief executive in the form of formidably advocating values and methods.

4 The deliberate and conscious management of symbols through the action of managers and leaders.

5 The creation of a critical mass of shared values among chief officers and Members.

6 Identification of the authority's core values through a consultative and representative process. The values are deeply rooted.

7 Adopting low profile strategies for the realisation of core values, and consciously avoiding a 'hard sell' approach.

8 Reviewing and monitoring the reward systems to ensure their alignment with the new culture. Concentrating on the more subtle forms of reward, not major incentive schemes.

9 Building rapport with key stakeholders so as to create allies not enemies.

This case study is included not as a prescription for others to follow, but because it draws together many of the issues raised in this chapter. Points 2 and 4 illustrate the importance of symbols in sending signals to the organisation. Points 7 and 8 deal with changes at the level of practices, and points 5 and 6 at the level of values. Issues of HRM practice (points 1 and 6), and of power (points 5 and 8) are also raised. Point 3, on leadership (one of the most significant factors at Wrekin) will be discussed in the next chapter.

CHAPTER REVIEW

This chapter has argued that in seeking to bring about cultural change, organisations need to address changes at the levels of:

- Symbols (missions, visions, expressions of management commitment, leadership).
- Practices (systems, structures, procedures, behaviours, allocation of resources, performance management and reward systems, monitoring and evaluation).
- Values (education and support for shifts in attitudes, values and orientations).

The chapter has pointed to the need to align HRM practices, structures and systems with the desired goals of change. It has also explored the interrelationships between values, resistance and power in the dynamic process of cultural change.

7

Leading change

- Explores approaches to leadership in local government.

- Describes success factors for leading cultural change.

- Provides questions for leadership teams to assess their capacity to lead a major change initiative.

- Outlines approaches to the management of change and uncertainty.

- Identifies strategies for managing transition.

- Explores motivation in times of change.

Leadership is one of the most important, but also one of the most elusive, requirements of cultural change. This centrality of leadership has made it something of a 'holy grail' of management, with hosts of textbook writers and consultants seeking to distil its essence and sell it on to others. This chapter has a less ambitious approach, based on exploring the characteristics of leadership in local government and drawing on descriptions by local authority chief executives and directors of their own approaches to leading change.

The local government context

In local government, there is no single model of good leadership. The skills required will depend on the culture and traditions of each local authority, its size, and the nature of the changes it faces. However, cultural change requires a more creative and intuitive approach than does traditional management:

> ... *strategic vision depends on an ability to* see *and* feel; *it cannot be developed by people who deal with little more than words and numbers on pieces of paper* (Mintzberg 1994 p. 270 [emphasis in original]).

Good leadership is more than good management. It requires vision, commitment, and excellent communication skills. However, leadership in local government is fundamentally different because of the pivotal importance of the officer/member relationship, and because of the divisionalised form of most local authorities. This makes leadership both a more *political* and more *fragmented* activity than in other sectors. Lines of accountability are complex, and the distinction between political control and strategic management remains ambiguous. Potential conflicts of culture and values between politicians, managers and professionals may make clear leadership difficult. A 'transformational' approach to leadership, then, may only be possible where there is a strong alliance between lead officers and members around an agreed change agenda. Whatever the approach, however, members must play an active role in providing leadership, both setting out and actively supporting the changes required.

The trigger for identifying a need for cultural change is often a change of political control. In some local authorities, shifting patterns of political control have resulted in periods of internal uncertainty and lack of direction. In others, changes in political control have been the stimulus for a period of re-evaluation leading to a sharper focus on purpose and values. This requires a 'shaping', 'enabling' and 'facilitating' leadership role by the chief executive, together with careful alliance-building amongst both officer and member groups. Once new agendas are in place, however, organisational leadership is required to carry through change. Different leadership approaches and skills, then, are required at different stages of the process. Coalition building, consensus seeking and agenda setting are required in the early stages, but once the direction is established, visible and public leadership is needed. Both 'backstage activity' and 'public performance' are required.

Many studies have emphasised that leading change must be seen as a collective and multi-faceted process. It is about sharing power as well as using power, and about drawing on multiple talents and skills. It needs to be more subtle and pluralistic than the 'heroic' imagery much of the business literature suggests:

> The tasks of leading change are about the resolution of a pattern of interwoven problems, not the tackling of single great issues. The problems of maintaining simultaneous action over a long term process are at their sharpest in leading change. The need appears to be not for boldness nor decisiveness, so much as a combination of planning, opportunism and the adroit timing of interventions (Pettigrew, Ferlie and McKee 1992 p. 279).

At the same time there is a need to recognise the symbolic and ceremonial significance of whoever is seen as 'the leader', whether this is chief executive officer, director, council leader, or team leader. What follows below is a summary of factors which 'leaders' in local authorities have identified as important in their personal approaches to leading change.

Leading cultural change: the success factors

Crafting the approach to change

Presenting staff or members with a highly structured 'grand plan' for change is not the most effective beginning. Focus instead on building agendas, developing the approach from broad-ranging discussions (between members, managers, staff and communities), and letting the overall direction emerge through a process of crafting and shaping.

Setting the overall vision and direction

Once the direction begins to emerge, there is a need to capture it in some kind of vision, mission, or statement of purpose. This needs to be presented and discussed in face-to-face meetings between chief executive or director and the staff group.

DEVELOPING POLICY NARRATIVES

It is important to sell change by drawing on the values, traditions and culture of a specific local authority. Policy narratives 'tell the story' of change in a way which:

– Links the past to the future.

– Is oriented around a value base of relevance to your audience.

– Links policy to practice.

Policy narratives depend on oral, not written skills; they should capture the imagination and engage the audience.

Creating the symbols

Leadership provides many of the symbols which give meaning to change. A leader who recognises his or her symbolic role will create ceremonies and events to celebrate achievements, will develop new stories, images, metaphors and so on, and will be physically present where it matters most.

The more radical and 'transformative' the change programme, the more important this type of symbolic leadership becomes.

SYMBOLIC LEADERSHIP

Creating narratives.

Articulating values.

Being visible.

Creating meaning.

Being aware of the symbolic importance of your own actions.

Changing the language you use.

Using time differently.

Paying attention to particular details.

Changing your own behaviour to model new values.

Responding to crises and problems in a different way (a way which reflects desired changes in values or behaviour).

Modelling new values and practices

Leaders serve as models of style, behaviour and values, whether they do so deliberately or not. One of the hardest lessons concerns the symbolic importance of a leader's own actions, which will be actively watched and interpreted by staff. It is the response to a specific event, the action at a given moment, the way in which a crisis is handled, that is given attention rather than the official statements. As a leader what you say matters: your words will be listened to very closely. But even more important is what you do: what you give attention to, how you make decisions, how you handle conflict, how you manage meetings, your use of time and other aspects of the minutiae of everyday behaviour.

WHAT KIND OF MODEL ARE YOU?

What do you give priority to in deciding how to allocate your time?

How much time do you spend out and about in your organisation?

Of the things that regularly go wrong, what did you last make a fuss about?

What words do you use most often when talking to staff?

How did you deal with the most recent crisis faced by your organisation?

When did you last praise someone?

What happened the last time someone in your own team made a mistake?

What kind of corporate or community events are you most likely to attend?

When you need to communicate with someone, do you tend to get your secretary to send a note or memo, talk to them on the phone, send an E-mail or go and find them?

What performance measures do you personally scrutinise on a regular basis?

What kind of people do you tend to favour when putting together project teams?

What kind of people do you like to surround yourself with on a day-to-day basis?

What kind of people do you 'mentor' on a formal or informal basis?

Which councillors do you communicate with regularly?

Create and celebrate success

When taking on a new leadership role, or embarking on a programme of change, it is important to demonstrate an early success, however small. Comments from directors include:

It is important to start where you are likely to have some wins.

Go in fast and demonstrate an early success, especially if this is on something that is regarded as difficult.

You need to win people's confidence in you and in your ability to deliver early on. If you leave it for too long, or are overcome by barriers too soon, you will never get another chance. This means it is important to have good information on what is likely to succeed , and to know who to trust to work with you on it.

It is important to 'talk up' the successes of the organisation as a whole, to celebrate achievements, and to mark significant transitional moments.

Our staff had been through hell while (a particular change) was going on. They worked all hours, and put up with physically very difficult conditions. We tried to keep them going by talking about what it was all for, and when it was over we celebrated. The reward element for staff was only token but it was appreciated because it provided some symbolic recognition of what staff had contributed.

We thought it was important to provide staff with the opportunity of celebrating our achievements in putting (a particular bid) together. Even though the bid was not successful, we wanted to celebrate the way in which the team had worked and its impact on the senior management group as a whole.

As we move towards local government reorganisation we want to find ways of celebrating the achievements of this local authority in the past in order to ensure that we recognise what we want to take forward into the new authority.

Communication

Effective communication is essential. Chief executives and directors commenting on this aspect of leadership talked about the need for simplicity, clarity and repetition:

Messages have to be simple and you have to keep repeating and reinforcing them. Don't overestimate what people can take in.

While most local authorities have introduced some form of structured mechanisms to improve internal communication (team briefings, internal newspapers and so on), many also emphasised the need for a personal touch:

I hold regular meetings with the top 100 managers.

Our Chief Executive has held regular open meetings on local government review for any staff who want to attend.

Trust is also seen as important:

Whenever I have made a decision to trust staff with information, although this has sometimes created difficulties (with members and/or with unions) it has always proved to have been the right course in the long term.

Most emphasise that communication is not just about sending messages to others; it is about ensuring that you receive them, and that those you do receive are truthful. As one chief executive commented:

People just don't tell you about the things that aren't working.

However, there is a good deal of frustration about how far it is possible to elicit feedback up the organisation. Team briefing has often not been well received, seeming to consist of messages from on high. Feedback is either not forthcoming or is highly edited as it moves back up the organisation. There is, then, a need for leaders to develop personal antennae down and through the organisation. But above and beyond that it means creating a climate of trust and openness to information and dialogue. This is more a question of personal style than of formal processes and systems.

Working with the grain of the organisation

One (female) chief executive talks of 'change by stealth'. Rather than challenging existing power bases openly by attempting to change the structure, it is possible to make massive changes through informal networks which cut across structures.

> Find out where the skills are and use them.

Unless you have an organisation which is in tune with what you are trying to do, it is unlikely that you wil be successful. This means that every formal change initiative must be based on getting people to rethink how to do things, not just what to do. It means influencing the norms of group behaviour. It means a change of emphasis from making decisions to selling changes, focusing on reinforcing, coaching, exhorting, championing, supporting and serving as a model. It means steering change through what John Stewart terms:

> . . . finding the right touch on the wheel.

In many organisations this 'incremental' approach may be more effective than grandiose schemes for change.

Overcoming the soggy sponge syndrome

The 'soggy sponge syndrome' is the phenomenon that swallows up the energy of change initiatives as they move down the various layers of the hierarchy, often being completely dissipated at middle management levels. This is usually not a matter of inertia, but is more likely to be a result of the challenge to vested interests and established territory that change brings. Ways in which this can be tackled include:

Sell change directly to those who deliver services, and involve them directly in working out new ways of doing things.

Get directors and other senior staff to champion specific change initiatives that they are not directly responsible for, in order to deal with barriers that are created.

There is sometimes a need to challenge people directly and make it very clear what is required of them.

Be very clear about what the objective is. Emphasise the outcome expected irrespective of the processes or professional boundaries which might be invoked.

You need managers who reinforce the new ideas at 2nd and 3rd tiers. Inform them about the need to shift their views, and reinforce this by being seen to do things differently yourself.

Energising change

Many managers tend to relinquish their personal involvement in an initiative once it is launched and plans reach the implementation phase; and it is here that many initiatives founder. Leadership is an important means of energising change. As one director commented:

Leadership is the physical momentum of change. Start with the conviction that organisational culture can be changed if you have the will and commitment to do so.

This may require selectivity to ensure focus: you can't be energetic everywhere at once.

Building commitment

Cultural change must be supported by leading politicians and by the whole of the senior management team. The key to success is the commitment of senior staff and councillors, and their ability to provide leadership. Real change will only take place if staff are convinced that it is needed, know what it is about, and are willing to support it. Having decided that some kind of 'transformational' change is needed, the next issues to consider are concerned with developing the leadership capacity to deliver it. The discussions here must be concerned with process as well as task, and a range of factors need to be considered:

Questions for management teams and member groups

Where do we want to get to?
(It is assumed that this will be based on input from politicians and managers)

— *What kind of organisation do we need to build?*

— *What is our vision of the kind of culture and values on which it must be based?*

— *What are our core objectives as a team?*

What steps do we need to take to get there?

— *What kind of change programme will be needed?*
(NB: at this stage the concern is with scale and scope rather than with setting out plans and programmes.)

Have we got enough commitment as a team to see this shift through?

— *Have we reached a consensus that change is needed?*

— *How much real commitment, as opposed to token agreement, is evident?*

What are our strengths and limitations as a team?

— *How effectively do we work together?*

— *Are we the right size?*

— *How useful are our meetings?*

— *How do we handle conflict?*

How might we need to change our structure/membership, and/or our working practices, to deliver the kind of change we want to see?

— *How well do we communicate?*

— *How visible are we?*

How effective is our current approach to providing leadership?

— *How would we evaluate our personal skills (individually or collectively) to lead change?*

– *Overall, does our current management team have the capacity to manage a major change initiative?*

A single leadership team, however effective, is not enough to carry an organisation through complex change. Local authorities need to develop and enhance the leadership capacity of the organisation as a whole, with a range of staff at different levels being developed to take on leadership roles. This is not as simple as it sounds: the sharing of power is often not an easy matter in local authorities with a strong corporate centre or charismatic central figure. Many local authorities will recognise the chief officer who insists on running a major change programme single-handed by working 60/70 hours a week, refusing to share responsibility. Many have responded to this by devolving responsibility down the organisation and by dealing with change initiatives through 'project teams' and the like. A shared approach to leadership is likely to enhance the overall capacity of an organisation or group to respond to change effectively. It can enable a local authority to draw on a much wider range of talents and skills throughout the organisation, including those of black and minority ethnic groups, of women, and of people with disabilities from whom traditional 'leaders' have rarely been drawn. It also enhances the capacity for organisational and group learning – a topic explored in the next chapter.

Managing uncertainty

Any large, complex change will result in periods of uncertainty and dislocation. This section offers a perspective on managing uncertainty, based on a study of managers in the NHS during the shift from passive administration to assertive management, and the introduction of market forces (Barrett and McMahon 1990). The study found that managers coped with uncertainty not by using sophisticated planning techniques, nor by increasing top down control. The emphasis was on negotiation and bargaining with a wide range of stakeholders, exerting influence rather than exercising managerial authority. This, it is argued, is because of the multiplicity of stakeholders (inside and outside the organisation) who can influence the outcomes of change in the public sector. Conflicts of values and interests are typically close to the surface, and so responses based on political skills are a vital ingredient of success.

The authors argue that public sector managers need to develop three types of stategic thinking to enable them to manage well in uncertainty: those of *setting direction, building consensus* and *managing conflict*. ... These are all highly pertinent in a local government context, and can be applied to the politics of the council chamber as well as to the micro politics of the organisation itself, though my primary focus here is on the organisation and teams of staff within it.

Strategies in uncertainty: directions

Conventional planning models become progressively less useful the larger the number of variables being considered and the greater the level of instability (whether stemming from national government, the local political context or from the wider community). Strategy must therefore mean establishing a sense of direction rather than attempting to exert control over detail. The focus is on performance against strategic aims, not conformance to procedures.

Establishing a 'sense of direction' is based on two interrelated components:

1 Establishing core values as a template against which operational decisions can be made.

2 Establishing an approach to steering and coordinating disparate incremental change. This is based on negotiating a decision-making framework (how and where different types of decision will be made), and building a shared understanding of the strategic direction in order to draw together the multiplicity of decision-making points.

Such an approach will help build the capacity of groups and of systems to deal with change throughout the organisation. Change will appear as more coherent and integrated, and decision-making can be devolved more effectively since staff will understand the frameworks within which they are working.

In times of uncertainty, when multiple or complex change is being experienced by an organisation, it is essential that managers are aware of how to steer change rather than attempting to control the detail of implementation:

STEERING CHANGE

- Establish core values and principles.
- Decide how decisions are to be made.
- Decide when and how to delegate decisions and to devolve responsibility.

- Do not assume that the messages of mission, vision or values are understood and endorsed.

- Maintain momentum and create networks.

- Recognise the need to 'champion' change from the top.

- Shape the outcome of small changes into an overall pattern.

- Create structured opportunities for learning and review.

Building consensus

Managers, members and groups of staff in an uncertain environment must think equally carefully about strategies for reaching consensus. The 'sense of direction' must be supported by a broad consensus within the organisation or group and this must be actively built rather than assumed. Where there are conflicts of interests and conflicting goals to be negotiated, it is more useful to attempt to build consensus around agreement about *process* rather than about *goals*. Barrett and McMahon emphasise that:

> ... it is not only direction that is important in times of uncertainty, but the process by which that direction is established (Barrett and McMahon 1990 p. 29).

This means drawing people into the process of direction setting, exploring with them the implications for decision-making processes, and devolving decisions about the best means of achieving the direction as far as possible. Time is a big issue here. Not all change can be delivered through highly participative processes. However, time spent in building consensus before decisions are finalised is likely to be saved at the implementation stage.

Managing conflict

Involving multiple interests and influences will not necessarily create consensus. Groups can reach a shared understanding of the issues without coming to an agreement about the way forward. The outcome must then be based on a process of discussion and negotiation. Where this is conducted with a degree of openness the result is likely to be more effective and to produce more support than if decisions are taken behind closed doors. Groups may agree to work in the same direction even if their values, motivations and intentions are different, although such alliances may be temporary and may not be sustained when a different issue is raised. The point is that consensus must be built, not assumed. Barrett and McMahon argue that where conflicting goals are present it is useful to concentrate on establishing principles and processes to which all are willing to subscribe.

STRATEGIES FOR BUILDING CONSENSUS AND MANAGING CONFLICT

- Concentrate on values not plans.

- Develop a framework for negotiation and discussion where interests diverge.

- Establish openness and trust in the communication process.

- Involve key groups and actors in the change process.

- Put most energy into the areas which are likely to be most productive.

Developing strategies for conflict is based on 'political mapping', using techniques such as force field analysis or stakeholder analysis. This involves identifying key actors, (groups, sub-groups or individuals), assessing their interests in the issue, and making judgements about their bargaining power. This enables strategies to be developed around a good working knowledge of the territory. The more uncertain the environment, the more important this becomes. In mapping, avoid assuming that initial reactions (digging in) represent the eventual stance – where conflict exists, it is important to look beyond the initial reactions and positions. Don't assume that temporary alliances are permanent. Be clear and open about the overall strategy. Fudge and inconsistencies now will create problems in the future. Above all it is important that conflict is seen as potentially creative as well as potentially disruptive. It is something which requires managing rather than eradicating.

Transition management

Managing cultural change is not simply about introducing new systems and procedures. It is about taking people through a *process* of change which may have far-reaching consequences for how they interrelate with the organisation. As one chief executive commented:

> *When introducing change, be aware that you are not just managing a task, but are managing the lives of people going through the process. There is a need to provide guidance, support and solace.*

Cultural change challenges many of the meanings people give to their working lives. Old certainties and established relationships are likely to be broken and new ones not yet in place. New problems arise for which there are no immediately available recipes for action. Value systems are challenged by new ideologies.

This means that people have to go through a process of letting go of the old before they can move on purposefully into the new. One model of this process (Bridges 1991) views transition as comprising three elements which may overlap and interact with each other. The first is a process of 'letting go' of old identities and ways of doing things. This may be accompanied by or followed by a 'limbo zone', characterised by a lack of clarity and high levels of uncertainty. This is both a source of change and opportunity (new thinking becomes possible as old constraints disappear) and of danger (confusion, overload, high levels of sickness, lack of trust and the possibility of new internal divisions). The third element of the model is that of new beginnings: the process through which new roles are adopted and new behaviours become embedded. The model suggests that organisations must manage all three phases of the process, not just concentrate on the last. That is, it is necessary to support people in 'letting go' of the old ways of doing things, and to carefully manage the disruptions of the 'limbo' period, as well as to ascribe new roles and set new goals to support the process of 'moving on'.

MANAGING TRANSITIONS

Letting go: helping the process

- Identify who's losing what.
- Accept and acknowledge the reality of subjective losses.
- Don't be surprised about what appears to be 'over-reaction'.
- Expect and accept the signs of grieving.
- Give people information again and again.
- Define what's over and what isn't.
- Mark the endings.
- Treat the past with respect.

Making the most of the 'limbo' period

- Redefine the change with new metaphors.

- Create temporary structures and systems to get through it.

- Strengthen inter-group connections to overcome isolation and strengthen overall organisational identity.

- Use a change group to manage and monitor the process and ensure they are accessible to those affected by the change.

- Capitalise on confusion by fostering innovation; enable people to generate and test new ideas, and take the ideas seriously (tell people what has happened to them).

- Restrain the impluse to push for premature certainty and closure.

Reinforcing new beginnings

- Be consistent.

- Ensure some quick successes.

- Symbolise the new identity.

- Celebrate success.

Organisations frequently focus only on the third process – specifying new roles and behaviours – and fail to pay attention to the first and second phases. Unless the process of transition occurs, and people really let go of the old, then change will not become 'owned' by staff and embedded in the organisation.

Motivation in times of change

Culture is the site in which people make meaning and through which they identify (or not) with organisational goals. The process of attachment is complex. However it is clear that change over the previous decade has led to radical challenges to traditional lines of identity within organisations, involving challenges both to how staff construct *notions of progress*; and to the *sense of social purpose* which has traditionally characterised local government. Each of these raises motivational challenges.

A sense of progress

Many politicians and professionals have had to relinquish – albeit reluctantly – the sense of progression which was based on confidence in the ability to solve social problems, in the benefits of technology, and more generally in continuous progress from an unenlightened past to an enlightened future. This sense of progress was also based on the assumption of growth – which might be fast or slow, with occasionally some losses or setbacks – but with an overall sense of forward movement. While for some the shift towards better management and a stronger governance orientation provides a new and dynamic framework for action, for others it seems a less than satisfactory substitute.

A sense of purpose

In the past those working in public services were able to operate within a framework of meanings about their role as 'public servants', with a (generally unexpressed) sense of purpose based on 'doing good' or 'benefiting society', offered in exchange for a certain status and security. In the 1980s we have witnessed the challenge to professionalism and the rise of market/business oriented identities. This is not a smooth transition, but embodies tensions and ambiguities between different forms of identity. In some cases we can see a reworking of 'old' ideas (e.g. of public service) in the new languages of 'quality', 'customers', and 'empowerment', and with words like 'community' gaining a new resonance in the 1990s. At the same time, however, the focus on cost constraints and value for money, together with the move towards contractual relationships, can lead to an impoverishment of purpose and a narrowing of motivational goals.

Some of the questions which need to be explored about staff's experience of change include:

EXPLORING CHANGING MOTIVATIONS

– *How far, and in what ways, have the values of staff and members actually changed as a result of external and internal change?*

– *How have relationships between members and managers changed?*

– *How have the relationships between the local authority and its citizens changed?*

– *How has people's experience of local government work changed in recent years, and with what consequences in terms of morale and motivation?*

– *What have been the effects of internal fragmentation and other structural changes for the loyalties, values and interrelationships of staff?*

- *How far have performance management and PRP actually influenced motivation?*

- *How has the 'psychological contract' between staff and the organisation changed?*

- *Has there been any shift towards greater instrumentalism in people's orientation to their work?*

- *How, if at all, has the balance between paid work and the rest of life changed? And with what consequences?*

- *How well are staff dealing with the pressure which constant change brings with it?*

Each of the factors underpinning these questions has significant implications for staff motivation and morale.

Meeting the challenge of motivation

What can local authorities do to support staff undergoing change and to foster commitment and attachment? Motivation theory in the 1980s and 1990s has been less than helpful since, in crude terms, it tends to rely either on the 'inspiration' of leaders (for example the 'Excellence' school of Peters and others), or the 'instrumentality' of targets, contracts and PRP (underpinned in part by 'expectancy' theory and 'equity' theory). The former depends on personal commitment and attachment; the latter on a process of exchange between employer and employee. If personal commitment and attachment is potentially coming unravelled as a result of change, is a new instrumentality enough to replace it? Perhaps it will succeed in delivering the performance requirements of some local authority services. However it may not be enough to provide a new sense of purpose, and is unlikely to provide the foundation for a positive process of cultural change.

What, then, can local authorities do?

1 Treat staff as more than cogs in a machine. In most areas of work, staff *are* the service, at least from the point of view of service users. It is, then, important to foster good practice, to invest in the workforce, and demonstrate commitment to good employment practices wherever possible.

2 Provide the kind of effective leadership which gives a sense of the purpose and meaning of change, rather than just creating a set of initiatives, action plans and tasks to be implemented.

3 Foster synergies by creating opportunities for cross-unit working, secondments, shadowing, project teams and multi-disciplinary working.

4 Balance the instrumentality of performance management and PRP with the motivational force of genuinely giving people more responsibility.

5 Operate reward systems in a way which respects and values staff's contribution and personal sense of worth. Recognise that not all aspects of an individual's contribution can be specified and measured.

6 Give positive rather than negative reasons for change wherever possible. 'Value for money' has rarely been a rallying call which has inspired and motivated staff.

7 Create new motivational forces by re-valuing the tasks: for example reshaping values around user orientation, community 'empowerment', and positive service goals.

8 Create cultures which support staff in risk taking and in working in new ways.

9 Find a new language for expressing public service ethos and purpose.

CHAPTER REVIEW

This chapter has stressed the importance of leadership to the success of cultural change initiatives. It has argued that:

- Leadership in local government depends on an effective political/ management interface. Members need to take on an active role in providing leadership.

- Leadership can best be understood as a collective and multi-faceted process.

- There are a range of success factors, but the role of leaders in modelling desired behaviours and attitudes is critical.

- Leadership in times of uncertainty requires setting direction, building consensus and managing conflict rather than top down control over plans and implementation.

- Leaders need to support staff in the process of transition by helping them to let go of the old, by managing the limbo period, and by helping them move on by reinforcing new beginnings.

■ Local authorities need to meet the challenge of motivation which may arise from shifts in local authority purpose and role.

Finally, it has explored the concept of leadership capacity and has provided a set of questions for senior management teams and member groups to assess their own capacity to lead change.

8

Developing a learning culture

THIS CHAPTER:

Looks at how a local authority can develop its cultural capacity to change and to learn from change. It:

- Identifies potential barriers to learning.

- Explores issues which arise in attempting to develop a 'learning culture'.

- Identifies ways in which local authorities can promote learning.

- Suggests the importance of 'processual' learning.

- Offers a framework to promote 'strategic' learning.

The challenges of change set out in Chapter 1 require local authorities to open themselves to new sources of learning. However a local authority may have excellent systems in place for learning from its users, citizens and staff about the effectiveness of its services and policies, but be unable to do much with the results because of its low capacity to make change happen. It may set in motion wave after wave of new initiatives, but find that nothing much actually changes because initiatives are not evaluated effectively and tend to just disappear when attention moves on.

Developing a learning culture, then, means not only opening channels of learning between the local authority and its environment. It means evaluating and learning from its own experience of change. However there is a great difference between collecting management information through performance review, and using this to learn from what has happened in the past as the basis for doing it better next time. In times of rapid change the need to deliver results today can push reflection and evaluation down the agenda. 'Preparing for tomorrow' means more than planning the next initiative: it means creating the cultural capacity to listen and learn, and to reflect and evaluate experience.

Much has been said about the need to create local authorities as 'learning organisations' (see, for example, Stewart and Clarke 1992). But what does the notion of a 'learning organisation' actually mean? Can organisations, as opposed to individuals, actually learn? The analogy which is often drawn on in depicting the 'learning organisation' is that of an organism such as the human brain (Morgan 1988). The process of learning is depicted as a process which begins by an organism being triggered by stimuli from the external environment (new experiences, new information). To make sense of these, the important stimuli must be selected out from the complexity which surrounds them; they are explored, and eventually a response is formulated and acted on.

There are some problems with the analogy:

- Organisations are not organisms, and there is no necessary presence of a single 'brain' which can go through the learning cycle.

- Stimuli are received at multiple points across an organisation, and their channelling to the strategic apex, where thinking is assumed to take place, is at best imperfect.

- Hierarchical structures mean that information gets distorted or blocked as it travels upwards.

- Internal fragmentation splits a local authority or department into small units, and separates functions across purchaser/provider divisions. This potentially closes channels of learning.

- New information technology or management information systems will never be a complete solution to opening out information flows. Indeed increasing the information flow may create new problems.

- Learning systems in organisations going through rapid and complex change can easily become overloaded, so that it becomes difficult to separate out clear links between events and their consequences.

- The process of selecting and exploring new data takes place in the context of existing organisational cultures, which provide barriers and create biases. Responses to change will tend to be based on prior assumptions, embedded in the culture, through which reality is filtered and complexity reduced to manageable proportions. Organisations may well then learn the wrong things.

- Different subcultures are likely to operate with different sets of cultural filters, and will interpret events in different ways. There will, then, be struggles between different perceptions and interpretations of new information, and different views of the appropriate response.

These factors suggest that organisations must be thought of in terms of political and cultural, as well as organic, models. Information flow in organisations is dissimilar to information flow between neurons in the human brain because the *processing* of information takes place in a political environment. There are, then, a range of political and cultural factors which impede the collection, interpretation and understanding of new ideas and information. People think, but there is no clear evidence that organisations do.

However, organisations can create opportunities for individuals and groups to engage in learning by facilitating the processing of new experiences and information. This can be done by:

- Creating structured opportunities and initiatives: workshops, learning sets, seminars, secondments.

- Ensuring that proper evaluations of all pilot programmes and initiatives are produced.

- Using facilitators to support learning through engaging with a team in process evaluation.

- Devoting time to evaluating past change as well as planning the future (for example through strategic review).

- Setting up groups which bring people together from different cultures, and with different knowledges and experiences, to work on projects and change initiatives. Action learning sets is one approach.

ACTION LEARNING IN KENT

Kent's 'Making Connections' programme for senior managers illustrates the possibilities of action learning. This was based on cross-function learning sets each facilitated by an advisor. The programme was launched with a formal input from the chief executive who set out a range of 'big issues' on which the sets might work. After two or three months each set was invited to make a submission to feed back what they had gained from the experience, and these were allocated to one of the chief officers, acting as a 'champion' for a particular topic and considering how the ideas and suggestions would be incorporated into the management systems of the organisation. The effectiveness of this programme depended on the organisation's willingness to invest in it and to support it. The outcomes have included a management newsletter which provides managers and staff with updates on the big issues facing the county; regular opportunities to hear directly from the chief executive and chief officers on their personal views of key areas of change; and a 'Managing transitions' programme to support staff through the process of change linked to local government reorganisation.

Learning from citizens and customers

Local authorities have, in recent years, developed a range of approaches for learning from service users and from the wider community in order to respond more effectively to changing patterns of need or demand, and to changing perceptions of the role of local government.

Initiatives to enhance communication with service users include the now established methods of customer surveys, customer feedback cards, quality audits, user panels and so on. One local authority commented that while each of these was of limited value on its own:

> ... the mosaic of communication helps us get the balance right.

There is a balance to be drawn between qualitative data, in which the user can have an active voice in shaping the agenda of service design and development, and quantitative data, which allows a local authority to compare its performance from a user perspective across a range of service areas, or to trace changes over time. There is a suggestion of the beginnings of dissatisfaction with large scale surveys, and a desire to experiment with more focused instruments which can yield richer data about specific areas of performance. There is also a strong desire in many local authorities to build closer links with local communities through decentralisation. Many are attempting to find ways of strengthening the Parish Council role, or augmenting the role of back bench members in other ways.

The first set of initiatives can be characterised as fitting with a 'consumerist' model of local authority purpose, while the second can be seen as an attempt to develop its responsivenes to citizens and communities. While most authorities draw on both, the differences are important, and the emphasis taken will depend a great deal on the pattern of political control. There may, however, be tensions between *consumerist* and *political* processes of learning.

Local authorities are now experienced in communicating with users and communities through a variety of consultative and advisory mechanisms.

Some key issues, however, need to be resolved to ensure that these processes are effective. These include:

- How can local authorities incorporate the results of direct feedback from users into the policy-making process and service design?

  A great deal of activity is taking place to get feedback from users. It seems, however, that not enough is being done with the results (other perhaps than the acquisition of filing cabinets).

- How can the strategic centre open up upward channels of communication and learning from the point of service delivery?

  Everyone now agrees that communication is vitally important. The emphasis is, however, still on 'top down' communication through newsletters, team briefing and so on. While the latter usually includes a formal provision for upward feedback, this is rarely seen as effective by staff. Potentially rich data resulting from learning at the front line of service delivery, or from work on a locality basis, is therefore wasted.

- How can local authorities take more effective account of diversity in the feedback mechanisms they use?

  It is, in principle at least, relatively easy to explore ways of getting closer to communities on a geographical basis. It is much more difficult to take account of the views of communities of interests which transcend geographical boundaries. As local authorities strive to respond to issues of concern to women, to black and other minority ethnic groups, to people with disabilities, to carers and other groups, they must find more effective ways of refining the tools and instruments they use to gather feedback from users and citizens.

What is all this to do with culture? It is self-evident that a local authority which is hierarchical, in which managers do not listen to or value the ideas of their staff, and which has a preoccupation with internal issues, will find itself unable to respond to change. More challenging is the idea that a local authority with a homogeneous culture will not be able to respond effectively to the heterogeneity of the cultures of its citizens and communities. Cultures give rise to particular 'mind sets' which may mean that individuals and groups cannot accept learning which does not fit with the existing cultural assumptions. This has particular implications for the possibilities of learning from change.

Learning from change

The emphasis must be on creating the cultural capacity to change, and to learn from change. In doing so, there is a need to consider both *post hoc* learning (the evaluation of outcomes) and *processual* learning. *Post hoc* learning is relevant in situations where it is possible to identify a point when change is over, and then undertake analysis and learning after the event. However, the cycles of successive and overlapping changes which now typify local government management make *post hoc* learning difficult, and there is a need to focus more and more on *processual learning* – learning about how change is impacting on people, systems and services while it is actually taking place. This allows the adjustment of plans, targets and goals to take account of shifts which occur during the life of a particular project.

Processual learning is based on a number of cultural features:

- Performance management processes must help staff to review, reflect and evaluate as well as to plan and initiate change.

- Customer feedback mechanisms must feed directly to staff providing the service, and must cover a range of features rather than focusing exclusively on complaints.

- The local authority must provide opportunities for staff in different parts of the organisation to learn from each other, from partners or stakeholders, and from practice elsewhere: in the public, private and voluntary sectors; and in other nations and cultures, whether in Europe or beyond.

- The local authority must find ways of learning from the experience and knowledge of individual local councillors.

- The officer and member groups must be prepared to learn from each other, and to identify and explore mismatches in their perceptions and interpretations of events.

- Management style must be one which enables staff to do new things, or to try new ways of doing existing things.

- Planning processes should be participative to draw on a wide range of knowledge.

- Information technology can be a powerful means of opening up communication, and involving people in direct links to the centre from the periphery, by-passing middle management (who often act as learning blocks).

- Managers and staff need up-to-date information about the potential consequences of their actions to help them in decision-making. Rapid feedback (using IT) about costs, quality and other performance measures generates a learning process which can be immediately fed into decisions about future actions.

- Rewards should be structured in a way which reinforces new learning.

- Structures should be adaptable so that they can be adjusted relatively easily and cheaply.

- Management style should be tolerant of mistakes but ensure learning from mistakes.

To support processual learning, 'double loop' learning must be included in the process of strategic analysis and performance evaluation, which is discussed below.

Strategic learning

Most local authorities acknowledge that they are weak at looking at what has been put in place and evaluating its effectiveness. This tends to produce a crisis management/firefighting approach to change. One of the key factors for success in managing uncertainty is the capacity of an organisation to evaluate its own management processes and to learn from its own experience of managing change. In the report on the 'Well Managed Local Authority' project (Leach et al. 1993), the authors stressed the importance of reassessment and continuous reappraisal. This meant the evaluation of new structures, systems and other change initiatives in the light of the changing circumstances, and modifying or changing them altogether if necessary. The authors went on to emphasise both the conceptual and practical difficulties this presented. Although most authorities monitored their performance, few had effective means of learning with regard to the broader issues of change.

This highlights the importance of developing a strategic review process. This can take place in different settings: member groups, directorate teams, departmental management teams, units and project teams. A strategic review process:

- Sets out what the issues and goals were (what were we trying to do?).

- Assesses what has been delivered (what have we achieved?).

- Assesses the strengths and limitations of the way in which it has been delivered (did we go about it in the best way?).

- Reflects on experience.

- Identifies how to move forward.

The 'learning cycle' is thus like the one in Figure 8.1.

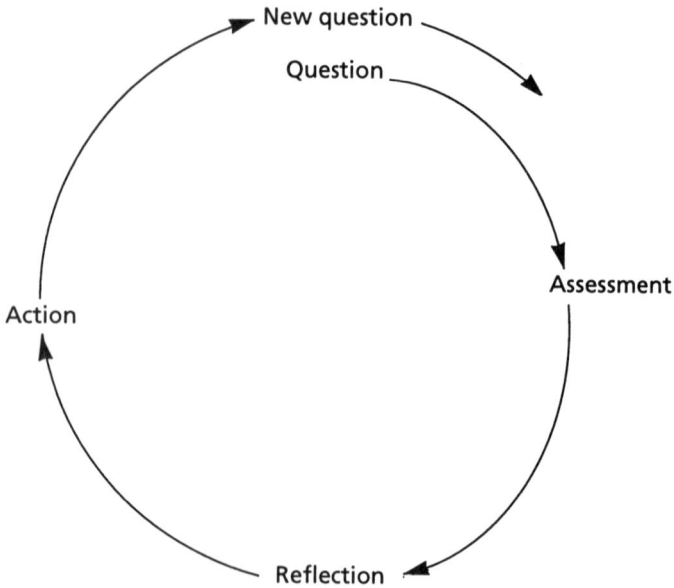

Figure 8.1

This cycle on its own only produces 'single loop' learning. That is, the wrong questions may be asked, or the analysis can be done in an insular way, thus reinforcing past assumptions. Reflection can be narrow, and so movement may be in the wrong direction. The process is made more productive where a separate review is conducted with other teams of staff or groups of members and the outcomes fed back into the review group. This serves as an important check on the perceptions of senior managers or members, and also opens the channels of communications so that the review process is strengthened, the learning loops enlarged, and the capacity for movement is amplified. The augmented learning cycle looks like that in Figure 8.2.

A similar expanded learning loop is possible with teams of staff involved in service delivery (whether to the public, to internal customers or external

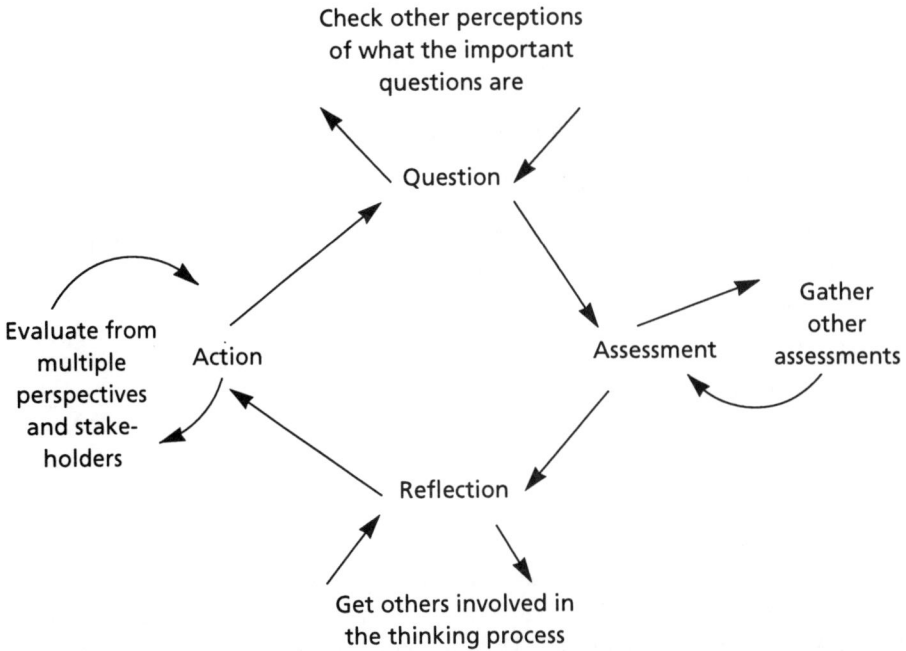

Check other perceptions
of what the important
questions are

Question

Gather
other
assessments

Evaluate from
multiple
perspectives
and stake-
holders

Action

Assessment

Reflection

Get others involved in
the thinking process

Figure 8.2

stakeholders), in which customer or stakeholder perceptions are gathered through survey, interviews or group discussions, and then fed into the self-evaluation process within the team.

Strategic review must include *process evaluation* as well as an analysis of results and achievements. The aim of any change programme must be twofold: to deliver the required outcomes, and in the process of doing so to enhance the organisation's capacity to deal with further changes in the future. This means setting out ways of evaluating the processes as well as the outcomes of change:

Outcomes

- Have we achieved what we set out to achieve?
- Did we begin with the right goals, or have more recent shifts (the goal posts changing) led to the need to reframe the original goals and plans?
- How effectively are new practices and procedures working?
- Has it made a difference to the end user?

⌐ Jcesses

- Did we do it in the best way?

- What have been the implications for staff, especially staff morale?

- How has the process of change been experienced by users (if at all)?

- What have been the consequences for intra-organisational relationships? (Have we reduced or enhanced the capacity of different parts of the organisation to work together?)

- What have been the effects on relationships with other agencies, partners and stakeholders?

Strategic review

The capacity to learn can be enhanced if senior managers and member groups engage with a process of strategic review in which opportunities for learning are explicitly identified. The following questions can be used as a framework for such a review process.

Strategic review questions: guidelines for use

- **Set aside time – this is a good 'away-day' activity.**

It is most effective if spread over at least two days with gaps in between during which development work can take place and be evaluated at the next meeting, or during which other evaluations can be set up and then fed in to the process.

- **Separate this activity from normal business.**

- **Establish some ground rules. These should be your own, but other groups have arrived at ground rules such as:**

- Don't push for early closure and decisions. You have to look backwards before you can look forwards.

- No going over old squabbles.

- Focus on the common issues.

- Focus on finding common principles rather than sorting out detail.

- Ensure everyone can get heard. (Lower ranking members and/or newer members often have the most useful contributions to make.)

- Honesty helps, blame hinders open discussion and learning.

Strategic review framework

1 How are we doing? (review)

- *What change programmes have we tried to introduce?*

- *What were our successes?*

- *Where might we have done things differently?*

- *How coherent do the changes seem?*

- *What lessons can be drawn from our experience that might help us in facing the next changes to come?*

'Double loop' question: have we got the review mechanisms in place that will enable us to answer these questions? If not, how can we develop them?

2 What issues do we face? (strategic analysis)

Assessing change

- *What external changes are on the horizon?*

- *What changes are taking place in key stakeholder or partner organisations?*

- *What changes are taking place in the communities we serve?*

- *What changes are taking place in user requirements?*

'Double loop' question: How effective are the mechanisms we use to assess external change, and how effectively do we use them?

Identifying uncertainties

- *What are the major areas of uncertainty we face?*

- *What alternative scenarios might we have to plan for?*

- *How can we monitor the changing pattern as it unfolds?*

'Double loop' question: How good are we at dealing with uncertainty? How do we tend to respond, and with what consequences?

Strategic issues

- *What are the strategic issues we must develop responses to? (i.e., where do we need to focus our time and energy?)*

- *What is their order of priority?*

- *What might we have missed?*

'Double loop' question: How can we check our perceptions of what the key issues are?

3 Where are we going? (strategic direction)

Developing a sense of direction

- *Are the values and purpose of the authority clear? and known to all?*

- *Do we have a sense of direction which can steer us through uncertainty and guide the change process?*

- *How can we achieve the goals we aspire to?*

'Double loop 'question: What changes might be needed in the way we work to achieve this?

Providing leadership

- *How effective are we in providing a sense of direction for staff?*

- *How effective are we as a leadership team?*

'Double loop' question: How can we evaluate our leadership styles, strengths and limitations?

4 How can we respond to emerging issues and problems? (making choices)

- *What concerns and issues are likely to arise in the foreseeable future?*

- *What are the key choices we will have to make in responding to them?*

- *How effective will our values and direction be in guiding these choices?*

'Double loop' question: How will we know whether we have made the right choices?

5 Have we got the skills and capabilities we need? (capacity building)

- *Are we developing the skills which we will need in the future?*

- *How effectively do we equip staff for change?*

- *Have we devolved responsibility to the right levels?*

- *Have we got the right kinds of structures and systems in place to support this?*

- *Are the internal and external networks strong enough to deal with complexity and to manage uncertainty?*

- *Where might we need to build new synergies to respond to emerging strategic issues?*

'Double loop' question: How will we know how well we are doing with regard to individual and organisational development?

6 What do we need to do? (change leadership and management)

Symbols

- *What signals do we need to send?*
    to customers and communities
    to staff
    to stakeholders

- *How can we model the new values and behaviours we want to embed?*

Practices and behaviours

- *What changes in organisational and individual behaviour are needed?*

- *How can we develop and reward new behaviours?*

Values and principles

- *How can we communicate the values around which change will be based?*

- *How can we link the values to practical principles to guide staff through change?*

'Double loop' questions: How effectively have we managed change in the past? How can we develop more effective approaches in the future?

7 How well do we evaluate our progress? (monitoring, evaluation and learning)

- *What do staff groups require to enable them to review their own progress?*

- *How can self-learning within staff groups be supported?*

- *How can we ensure that learning is fed back into the whole organisation, and forms the basis for future action?*

- *How will we know whether we are learning the right things, not the wrong things?*

— How can we develop the learning capacity of staff, of teams and of the organisation as a whole?

Developing learning capacity

Evaluation and learning are perhaps the weak links of the change management process in most local authorities. While chief executives, members and senior managers are well able to reflect on their experience and draw lessons from it, there is little evidence that this type of learning is built into organisational processes and review mechanisms. There is much talk of the 'learning organisation' but little real evidence of its existence. Perhaps there is now so much emphasis on continuously moving forward that it is difficult to look back; decisions are always urgent, and stopping to think and reflect is a luxury. Local authorities are becoming information heavy, but are not developing their capabilities of using information effectively. Key issues are:

■ Drawing on learning from users, citizens, councillors and front line staff into the policy and strategy process.

■ Fostering a learning process across organisational boundaries.

■ Building learning into the process of managing change.

CHAPTER REVIEW

This chapter has argued that:

■ Local authorities are becoming information rich without developing their capacity to make effective use of information by engaging in learning.

■ Local authorities cannot easily be thought of as learning organisms. There are a range of political and cultural factors which potentially impede the collection, interpretation and understanding of new ideas and information.

■ The learning process needs to be actively promoted through structured opportunities and initiatives.

■ In gathering data from users and communities, there may be tension between consumerist and political processes of learning.

- The management of change needs to be supported by processual learning as well as the evaluation of outcomes.

- To support this, 'double loop' learning needs to be included in the process of strategic review.

In developing a 'learning culture', the ideas of *process evaluation*, developing *learning capacity*, and *strategic learning* have been explored.

9

Strategy, culture and change: a question of balance

THIS CHAPTER:

- Highlights strategic tensions which arise in the process of local government change.

- Provides a diagnostic questionnaire to indicate the current cultural balance within a local authority or department.

- Suggests strategies for managing some of the tensions.

External pressures have forced local authorities to develop new kinds of organisational structures and arrangements through which costs can be contained, and through which greater levels of flexibility and responsiveness can be delivered. The degrees and extent of these changes have been enormous, and the achievements impressive. But there is now, perhaps, a need for a reassessment of the patterns which have emerged, and a consideration of how to achieve a better sense of 'organisational balance' in response to the dilemmas of change.

In the kind of contexts in which local authorities are now operating, simple recipes for managing change are less than helpful. Different pressures for change require different forms of cultural adaptation, and not all are compatible. For example the pressure to be more 'flexible' may well be in tension with the pressure to retain strong lines of political accountability and to meet government performance targets, both of which require strong internal controls. Similarly the pressures to be more ' businesslike' may be in tension with demands to respond to long-term community agendas.

Different ways of resolving these tensions have implications for what I term 'organisational balance'. This chapter explores some of the key issues emerging from work with a range of local authorities, and identifies ways in which some are attempting to address imbalances which have arisen.

Identifying the issues

The internal tensions arising from change are expressed in different ways in local authorities, depending on their culture and history, political choices and priorities, and on the ways in which change has been managed. Some of the main dilemmas are outlined below.

Corporatism/departmentalism

Chapter 1 discussed the shifts which have led local authorities to develop greater external awareness, and responsiveness both to service users and to wider community issues. Tensions between these can be expressed in the form of tensions between the corporate centre (increasingly concerned with corporate change agendas which transcend departmental areas of interest) and service departments issues (with an emphasis on specific service users).

Corporatism/departmentalism is perhaps the classic tension which has arisen from the historical pattern of development of local authorities along departmental lines, linked to professional power bases. In recent years, this tension has tended to increase for two reasons. One is the need for financial stringency, which has driven the corporate centre to exert stronger fiscal controls over departmental working. The second is the shift in many authorities towards a 'community governance' agenda, together with the shift towards an 'enabling' role in service delivery.

The development of a more corporatist approach at the centre is, however, meeting resistance from departments. In one authority, departments had a great deal of autonomy, and there were wide differences in approach on key issues. There was considerable tension between the role of the centre and of departments, expressed in terms of the centre's imperative to run a corporate organisation and the desire of departments to control what they do. The centre–periphery tension was expressed as conflicts over the view of organisational purpose:

> On questions of what is our business, and what is the best way of doing our business, each department would have its own style and would answer differently.

The more customer oriented departments were especially resistant to the building up of power at the centre. The centre–periphery tension is seen as one between responsiveness to customers versus the development of corporate agendas:

Those parts which touch the customer are doing it right. We know what business we are in. The centre doesn't.

The very strength of the customer focus which had been developed in the mid/late 1980s, strongly influenced by the 'excellence' approach, had perhaps become a barrier to the development of a 'governance' approach to community concerns. In this authority a debate emerged about the disbenefits of the strong departmentalism, but at the same time there was resistance to changing it. However, the divisions were softened by the strength of the organisational culture, which acted as an integrating factor. Interdependencies were acknowledged and valued:

Each department is seen as self sufficient and as looking after its own interests. But it is unthinkable that we would do anything to degrade another department. The bottom line is that if I was going under, I know that others would support me.

Decentralisation/centralisation

In many local authorities, the development of a stronger corporate approach at the centre is taking place in the context of the redefinition of the role of traditional service areas, with greater degrees of decentralisation and an increase in multi-disciplinary working through the development of 'one-stop shops', multi-disciplinary project teams and so on. In some cases this is seen as good preparation for local government review, which would, it was hoped, merely result in changes to the ways in which area teams were managed, without disturbing their internal functioning.

In one authority, one-stop shops were now well established. In the early days, they had been the focus of considerable inter-departmental tensions. As the shops became embedded, however, new tensions arose between the areas and the 'home' departments:

It's more like them and us now. They (the departments) don't like the fact that we have our own budget.

The creation of areas inevitably sets up centre/periphery tensions.

Decentralisation, then, is rarely a smooth process (see Burns, Hambleton and Hoggett 1994). As well as centre/periphery tensions, decentralisation sets up tensions between multi-disciplinary working and professional forms of control. The Liberal Democrat leader of one authority commented that his party would want more decentralisation and devolution than the authority would accept, because it was still professionally based and departmentalised rather than multi-disciplinary and multi-service based. Rather than units oriented to a discrete part of the business, he envisaged multi-disciplinary town or area managers with lots of delegated powers, linked to area committees, but saw professional structures as operating as a barrier to this form of working. This raises a number of important questions about the role of professionalism in multi-disciplinary patterns of working; and about the development of managers and staff for jobs which transcend professional boundaries.

Flexibility/control

The search to develop more flexible and responsive organisations has resulted in increased devolution of responsibility to operational managers and to 'business units'. This sets up possible lines of tension between the 'centre' (representing corporate interests and member control) and the 'periphery' (business units or departments desiring maximum operational freedom). The limits to the freedom of operational managers with devolved responsibilities are still being worked out as local authorities learn from experience. Examples included:

Mistakes happen with devolution. What is important is to know why they happen, and to set clear guidance and control parameters – e.g. on contact with members.

The downside of devolution is that you have to centralise as well as decentralise.

We had a little trouble with some contracts, which has made people nervous. We recognised that not all were equipped to deal with contracts, and produced a handbook (an 'idiot's guide') on contracts linked to a mini lecture tour for staff.

A group of staff set up a company to market (a successful product developed for in-house use) and got their fingers burned. But bad lessons make it easier to accept some controls.

One department had radically changed its senior managers, promoting younger people with ideas to senior levels:

We believe in drawing on talent. We allow people to take responsibility when they are ready for it, but this means also allowing them to make mistakes. . . . Managers are given the freedom to manage, make mistakes and learn from them.

This kind of comment could be straight out of any private sector management handbook. However, the follow-up comment in the interview with the same manager points to the limitations of this in a public sector context:

But committee members find this (allowing staff to make mistakes) hard. The leader has said 'Any mistakes are too many mistakes for me'.

The flexibility/control tension which accompanies devolution highlights the need for effective monitoring and evaluation. The balance between too much and too little monitoring is difficult to achieve:

> No one follows things up to see if they are implemented.

> Some business plans have too many indicators. We don't meet any of them because we can't meaningfully monitor them, and we can't do anything with the results.

> We are good at innovation but not at follow up. For example when we analyse customer surveys, we are not always honest – we only want to hear the good news.

> We were good at getting the (one-stop shops) running, but not at monitoring what they do, so there are different standards across the shops.

The reorganisation of local authorities around business unit structures has in many cases resulted in a weakening of departmentalism. However it has also tended to result in excessive fragmentation and the loss of organisational synergies, and some authorities now feel that the restructuring into multiple units has resulted in an organisation which has become too internally divisive and competitive. This has been exacerbated by the structure of service level agreements and internal charging:

> Having been given large levels of freedom and responsibility, units inevitably want more.

Internal fragmentation into business units or multi-disciplinary area teams has implications for performance review and budget review. Members require a coherence for the reporting process which was not enabled by the pattern of internal divisions, especially around purchaser/provider splits:

> . . . there is an issue of where accountability lies – this is hard for members to understand.

Although monitoring and evaluation has been an enormous growth area in local authorities in recent years as a result of the Audit Commission and other external agencies, there are a number of questions about its value as an internal tool. There seems to be some lack of clarity in many authorities about how much to monitor, for whose benefit, and how to use the results.

Delivering results today/development for the future

In one authority, performance management is seen as an enormous success and was greatly appreciated by staff because it gives people responsibility. On the other hand, it is acknowledged that the changes have led to a very lean organisation with a lot of pressure:

So much has changed in the local government world. The pressure has increased; both the downward pressure on resources and the upward pressure on things to do. . . . We have achieved a lot, but haven't always resourced fully the changes we are making, As a result it tends to be a relatively small number of people who take everything on, and they are now very tired.

There is more to be positive about than negative about; but sometimes we work ourselves too hard. There may be a disaster around the corner – things may go wrong because too much is being carried out at once.

We put a lot of pressure on key people, and don't have enough time for reflection.

The extremely lean structure means that the expectations of what officers deliver is not sustainable. We may now have to make a choice about how to cut services because the stress on people is getting too great.

Flatter structures and fragmented organisational arrangements also have implications for staff development and for a longer-term strategic awareness:

There are risks that unit staff will just pursue narrow interests, and not get involved in wider projects.

We need people with a wider view. But this gets harder as people become more specialised, and as central units become redefined as support services. More complex organisations need a wider view – we need to consider how we are providing for this and preparing unit managers and staff to take on roles with a broader function.

DSO [Direct Service Organisation] managers are under-represented in corporate tasks – they can't do it because of the pressure they are under.

Our structure has become too flat. Units only have one or two people who understand the wider business.

People who are good at driving things find it hard to do strategy, to be reflective, and to develop a team approach.

Initiative doesn't seem to go with a team approach.

Our culture is very proactive, and one which values 'getting on with the job'. But this means that we are sometimes not reflective enough; and the Directorate team is perhaps not strategic enough.

Too many managers are activists, dealing with the issues of today, so don't consider how to prepare people for tomorrow.

This tension between 'results today' and 'development for tomorrow' is perhaps one of the most critical questions of balance to emerge from the research I have drawn on for this chapter. The focus on results has led local authorities to develop more fragmented structures and more devolved responsibility but with a limited focus defined largely by short-term goals. This has implications for organisational and personal development. Individual development requires staff to adopt a wider focus and develop a broader skill base than those required for doing the job today. Both organisational and individual development require career development paths which transcend the often narrow specialisms and focus of a particular business or service unit. Organisational development, and the management of complex change, require strong internal interconnections and the development of synergies through which the value of the whole can become more than the sum of the parts. These are critical issues for the future.

Mapping the tensions

The key tensions discussed above can be mapped using the matrix in Figure 9.1:

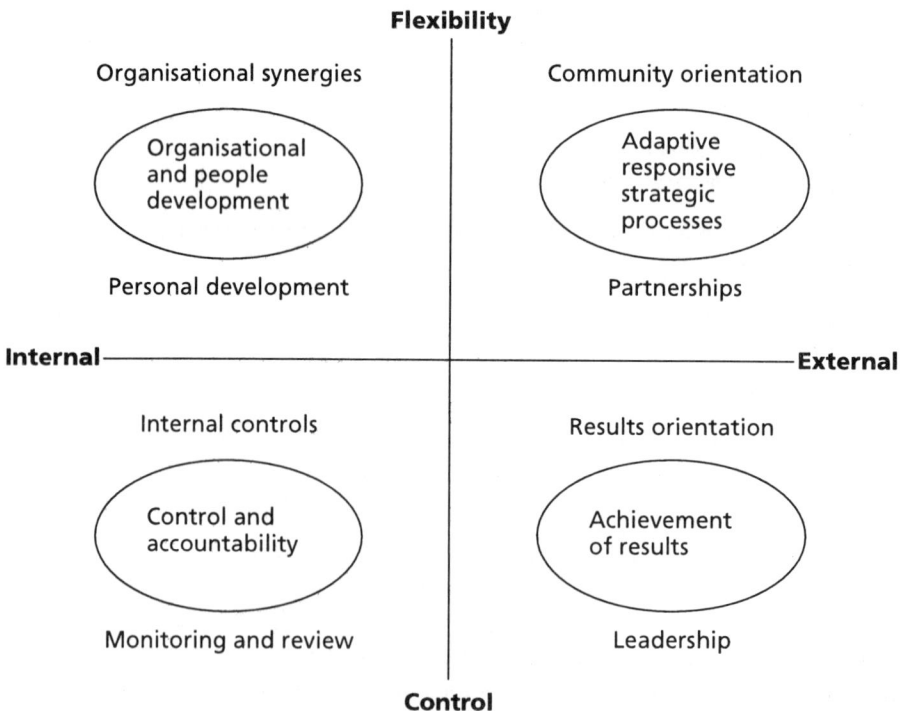

Figure 9.1   The strategy and culture matrix

Two key lines of tension emerge from the analysis: those between flexibility and control; and between fragmentation and integration. These operate between the diagonally opposite segments shown in Figure 9.2:

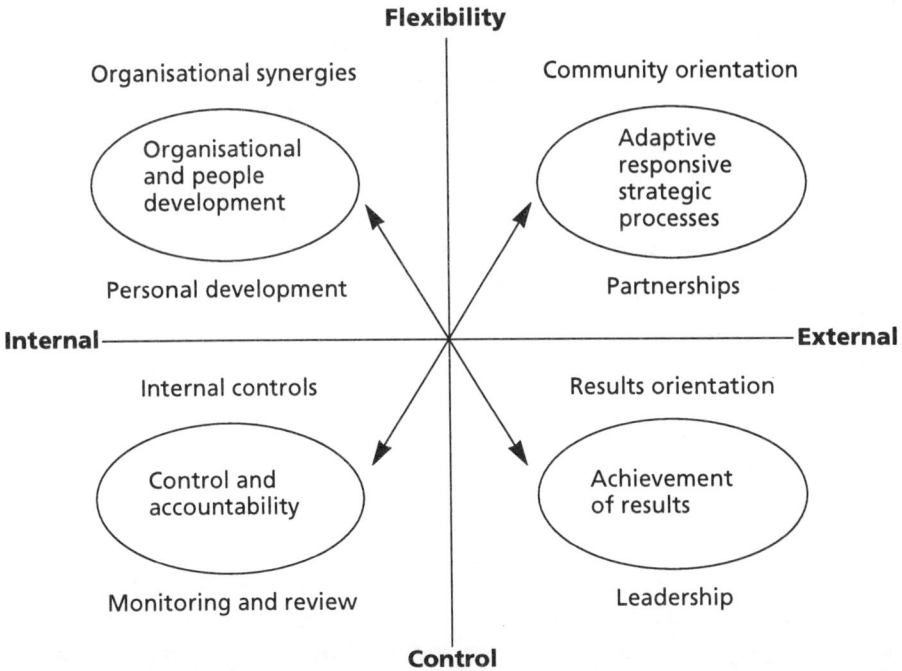

Flexibility

Organisational synergies   Community orientation

Organisational and people development

Adaptive responsive strategic processes

Personal development   Partnerships

Internal ——————————————— **External**

Internal controls   Results orientation

Control and accountability

Achievement of results

Monitoring and review   Leadership

Control

Figure 9.2   Mapping the tensions

They take different forms in different authorities, and are expressed in different ways depending on the overall purpose and goals of each. In those with a strong consumerist or neighbourhood orientation, flexibility will be a dominant organisational requirement, and the balance between flexibility and control must be carefully judged. In those developing a 'community governance' role, internal synergy becomes a critical issue so that the authority as a whole can respond to issues which transcend the interests of particular units or departments. All authorities, however, have to balance both sets of tensions.

Strategy and culture: diagnostic questionnaire

To help you to identify the kind of balance which has been achieved in your authority, you may wish to try completing the questionnaire below. Before doing so, three important points must be made:

1 The questionnaire is about perception not fact, and different people will perceive things in different ways. Generally the lower down the hierarchy a respondent is positioned, the more they will tend to see the balance as more towards control than towards flexibility.

2 The tool is indicative rather than conclusive. The results may suggest areas to explore further, rather than giving firm answers. Because of this, it is most valuable when used by a team, for example a management team. Different perceptions can then be compared. Where there are high levels of similarity, this may indicate issues which the authority will have to address. Where there are high levels of disagreement, this may indicate something about the team itself. Whatever the result, useful discussions generally follow.

3 The focus is on a local authority as a whole, rather than a specific department or unit, and respondents need to have sufficient feel for the corporate whole to make meaningful responses. The questionnare can, however, easily be adapted for departmental use.

The questionnaire

This is a diagnostic tool designed to assess the balance of forces at play in the interface between strategic leadership and organisational culture. Listed below are a series of statements. Please indicate how far you agree with each. Base your answers on your own perceptions of the effectiveness of your local authority on each dimension.

QUESTIONNAIRE

Use the following scale:

(1) Disagree strongly.
(2) Disagree.
(3) Neither agree nor disagree.
(4) Agree.
(5) Agree strongly.

1 This organisation has a strong community focus.

2 Senior managers are good at building effective bridges to stakeholders.

3 Our strategic planning process is effective in helping us focus on what's really important.

---

4   There is clear leadership which sets direction from the top.

5   Short-cutting proper procedures tends to be frowned upon and people who do so are penalised.

6   Reviewing performance against goals and objectives is now established practice throughout the organisation.

7   Staff from different parts of the organisation have regular opportunities to share ideas and work together in teams or groups.

8   The organisation values participative modes of decision-making.

9   We have developed effective ways of involving users in the design and evaluation of services.

10 We have developed strong strategic partnerships with other agencies.

11 We tend to be very good at achieving what we set out to achieve.

12 Our senior management/director team works effectively.

13 Individual accountabilities and lines of responsibility are crystal clear at all levels.

14 When we set up projects or pilots, we have effective ways of learning from both our successes and our mistakes.

15 Corporate loyalties tend to be stronger than professional loyalties.

16 Equality of opportunity for staff is taken seriously and actively pursued.

17 We have effective ways of seeking and responding to the views of diverse groups of users (such as women, black and ethnic minorities, people with disabilities and other groups).

18 Staff at all levels tend to be comfortable working across boundaries with other organisations.

19 Our performance management systems are effective in helping us to meet our short term objectives.

20 This organisation effectively communicates its goals and priorities to staff.

21 We are all very cost conscious here.

22 There is a lot of emphasis on setting individual targets and reviewing individual performance.

23 Departments tend to view the centre as 'adding value' to their work (i.e. as more of a help than a hindrance).

24 The organisation has effective staff development practices.

25 We have decentralised services to localities and redesigned services around user needs (e.g. through 'one-stop shops').

26 We have built strong links within the European Community and/or other international bodies.

27 The organisation is subdivided into units, each responsible for its own business or service plan.

28 We are good at celebrating our achievements.

29 What goes on in departments and units is strongly controlled by the centre.

30 As a management team, we regularly review our activities against our strategic goals.

31 There is a large degree of consensus around corporate values and goals, whatever department or unit staff work in.

32 This organisation cares about its staff.

Scoring the responses

First add up the total score for each of the following dimensions:

Community orientation   (questions 1, 9, 17, 25)

Partnerships   (questions 2, 10, 18, 26)

Results orientation   (questions 3, 11, 19, 27)

Leadership and direction   (questions 4, 12, 20, 28)

Control/accountability   (questions 5, 13, 21, 29)

Monitoring/evaluation   (questions 6, 14, 22, 30)

Internal synergies   (questions 7, 15, 23, 31)

People development   (questions 8, 16, 24, 32)

Then transfer your scores to the map by putting a dot at the appropriate point on the grid below for each of your totals. For example, if you have scored 12 for community orientation, put a dot on the radial line corresponding to community orientation at a position almost half way between the circles marked 10 and 15. Repeat for each of the other scores; then join all the dots together. You should come up with a diagrammatic representation of how you perceive the current balance in your local authority, as shown in Figure 9.3.

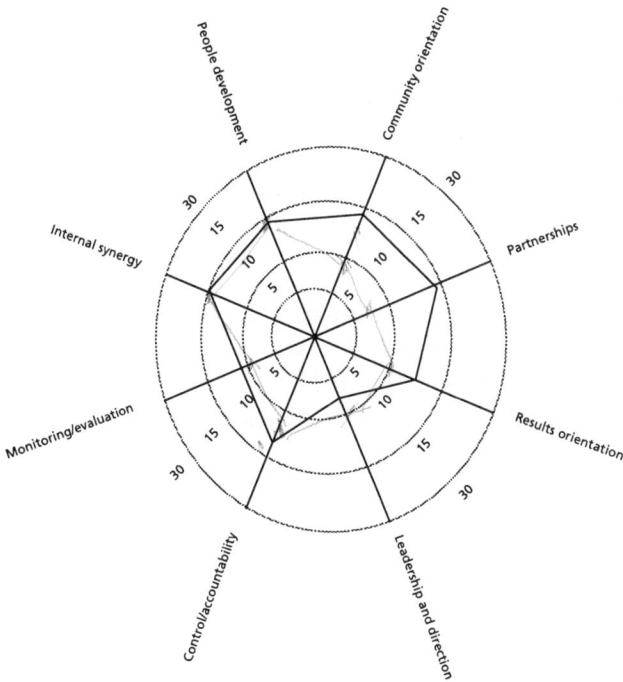

Figure 9.3 Mapping the results

Explore the overall pattern, looking at:

(a) the size of the outline you have drawn. A small shape, derived from low scores on most or all of the dimensions, suggests a perception of an undeveloped or impoverished culture. A large shape suggests a perception that the local authority is well developed in most or all of the dimensions explored.

(b) the shape of the outline you have drawn. High points and low points indicate well developed and poorly developed dimensions. Where a high point corresponds to a low point in the diagonally opposite quadrant, this may suggest that the organisation as a whole is out of balance.

Before reaching any conclusions, ask yourself whether the results feel about right. Remember, this is a matter of perception, not scientific fact. Then compare your results – the shape you have drawn – with those of others in the group if you are doing it with others in your team.

Some typical shapes that have resulted from use of the questionnaire:

Fig. 9.4: A traditional local authority with strong bureaucratic controls.

Fig. 9.5: A traditional local authority which has developed a strong community and/or customer orientation.

Fig. 9.6: A local authority which has developed strong community orientation and which has a cohesive internal culture; but which does not have the mechanisms to achieve some of its goals and which does not effectively monitor what it has achieved.

Fig. 9.7: A very business oriented culture with strong external partnerships, in which devolution works effectively (so controls are not felt to be excessive); but in which internal fragmentation and competition have led to a lack of internal synergies, and in which people development is felt to be weak.

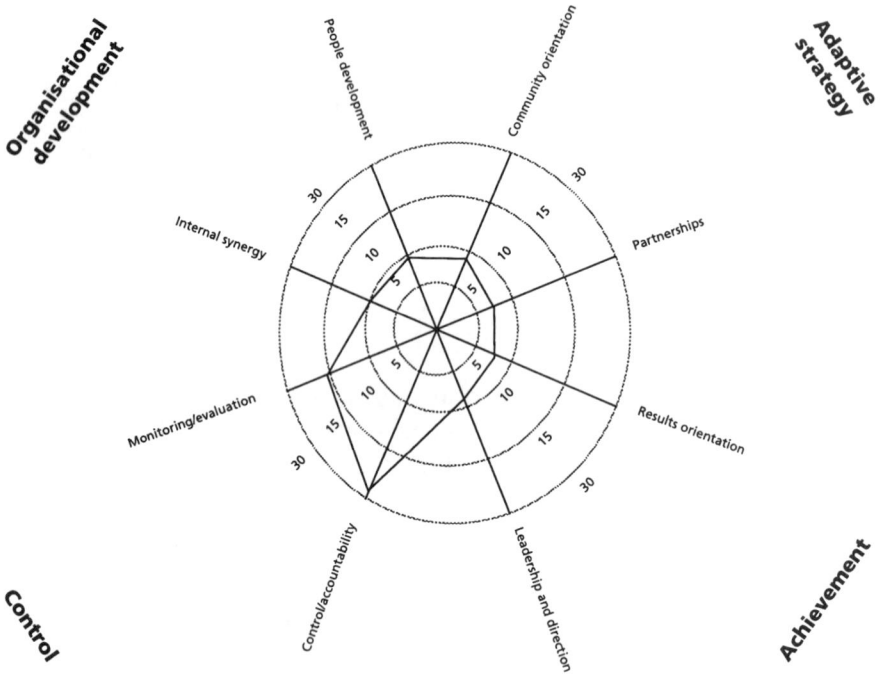

Figure 9.4   Traditional with strong bureaucratic controls

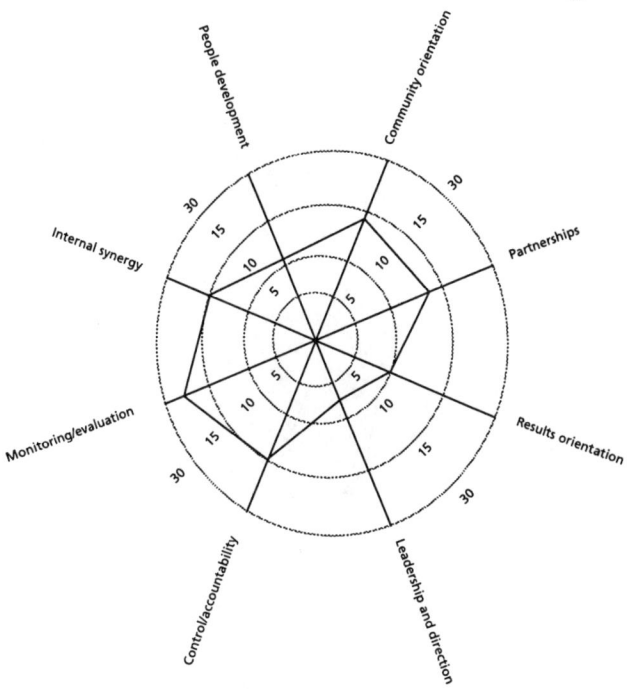

Figure 9.5 Traditional with community orientation

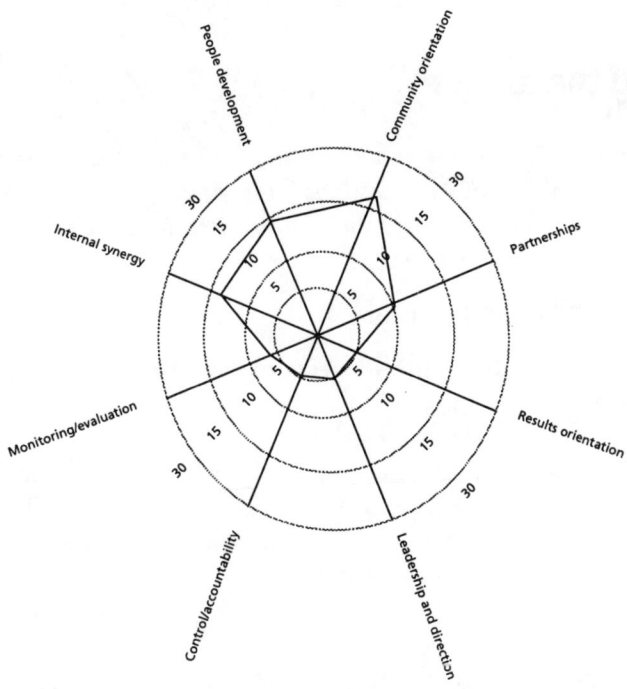

Figure 9.6 Community orientation and strong internal culture

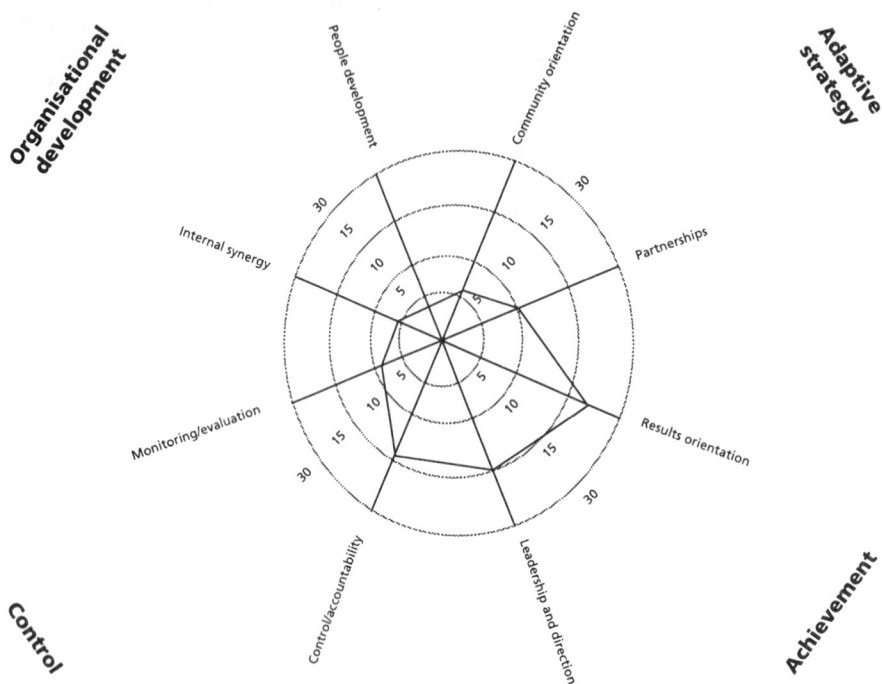

Figure 9.7   Business orientation and partnership approach

Managing the tensions

This section focuses on exploring responses to imbalances between opposite quadrants: between flexibility and control (top right, bottom left); and between fragmentation and integration (bottom right, top left).

Balancing flexibility and control

- **Identifying clearly the degree of freedom or autonomy for departments, units or areas**

In one authority with high levels of decentralisation, the management task to overcome these tensions was seen as improving communication between the centre and the areas so that the centre gave area teams the authority and the responsibility to get on with it; and so that areas know the priorities of the centre.

- **Setting standards and guidelines, identifying accountabilities and monitoring and reviewing performance**

In one local authority with high levels of devolution there have been a range of attempts to balance unit freedoms with central controls, through the introduction of corporate standards on issues such as training and development, pay and conditions, health and safety, contracts, internal purchasing, customer care, and support for councillors.

Balancing fragmentation and integration

Overcoming internal fragmentation depends on integrating the work of individual departments and units, making connections between them and developing relationships between different kinds of activity, so that the whole becomes more than the sum of the parts. Strategies include:

- Grouping business units or services within multi-function Directorates, or developing common 'Programme areas' or initiatives which bring together activities in different departments.

- Fostering cross-departmental working through task groups and project teams based around corporate change agendas, with individual directors or chief officers taking on roles as 'champions' of corporate change initiatives.

One local authority organised into multiple business units has attempted to build organisational synergies in a number of ways. Unit managers and all directors meet every two months to discuss current corporate issues. Unit managers are involved in implementing the Corporate Business Plan; individuals take responsibility for particular aspects of the plan based on their responsibilities, skills and interests. Cross-organisational learning is encouraged by the use of in-house expertise. For example, the learning of DSO managers had been drawn on when the rest of the organisation came to produce business plans.

New corporate initiatives are each headed by a lead unit manager, who is responsible to a named director. Each director thus has a portfolio of initiatives which transcend professional or departmental boundaries. For example, the director responsible for leisure is a key player in Investors in People strategy. Progress on these is linked directly into the performance management system.

- An important aspect of synergy building is that of addressing internal competition arising from business unit structures and purchaser/provider splits.

In one local authority, a recent change of political control, plus a period of reflection on the early successes and a realignment of thinking about the future, has led to a number of interesting shifts. One is the production of a regulatory framework to cut out internal competition between business units. The newly established Corporate Resource Department, which plays the central purchasing role, advises on functional resource policies such as personnel, and ensures that these policies are executed within corporate standards. These standards provide a clear framework within which units must work on issues such as personnel, property, public relations etc. It also fulfils a role of regulator of the internal market.

Another symbolic change has been a shift in ways of viewing organisational divisions and inter-organisational relationships: for example, the desire to view purchasing/providing roles as based on partnership rather than the pursuit of conflicting interests, and a change of language to one of partnership. This reflects a broader reassertion of a stronger public service ethos:

> We are having to struggle against the 'mythical' view of the role of a commercial manager – to deal with old prejudices in a new form.

> Devolution and the growth of professional services within departments had led this authority to identify the need for a 'Head of Profession' role at the centre, which bridges the purchaser/provider divide and 'helps staff to feel they are part of a wider family.'

Local authorities have adopted methods which illustrate different approaches to developing internal synergies. In some, centre–unit relationships have developed on a *contractual* basis, primarily through performance management systems; others are moving towards a more *regulatory* framework for the management of internal relationships. But real integration and synergies only really stem from building and fostering a common culture which can span internal lines of differentiation. Such a common culture (albeit one which values flexibility and diversity) is the foundation from which a local authority can respond to the broad community issues and governance agendas identified in chapter 1, and develop its future role and purpose.

CHAPTER REVIEW

This chapter has argued that:

- The process of strategic change can result in organisational imbalances expressed in a local authority's culture.

- Key tensions exist between:

  - corporatism and departmentalism;

  - centralisation and decentralisation;

  - flexibility and control;

  - results today and development for the future;

  - fragmentation and integration.

- In managing the tensions there may be a need to direct attention to internal integration, synergy building and organisational development.

- Getting the balance right is vital to prevent an overly fragmented culture and to build the capacity to respond to broad community issues and governance agendas.

10

Cultural change and cultural renewal

THIS CHAPTER:

- Discusses the relationship between externally imposed cultural change and internally led change and renewal.

- Explores value conflicts at the heart of the process of renewal.

- Highlights the importance of management approaches and styles in the process of renewal.

Most of this book has been concerned with cultural change. This chapter argues that following the prolonged period in which local government has been reacting to externally imposed change, attention now needs to focus on cultural renewal and the development of cultural resilience. There is a need to focus not just on change, but on the qualities of local authority cultures which it is important to sustain and foster. The old cultures of bureaucracy, paternalism and professional power have rightly been challenged. But what should replace them? Is the new ethos of 'consumerism' and 'business management' enough? There is a need to redefine local authority role and purpose, and to provide a positive sense of purpose and meaning for local authority staff. This chapter explores a number of political and management issues which are at the heart of this process.

Local government, cultural change and cultural renewal

Throughout the 1980s the idea of cultural change became something of a double-edged sword for local authorities. Many have been highly successful in pursuing internally led change in order to make their organisations more open, responsive, and user-centred. At the same time, however, cultural change became linked with the New Right project to transform the public sector and challenge the power of professional cultures. This was accomplished both through radical restructuring processes ('contracting out', purchaser/provider splits, self-governing trusts and grant-maintained schools), and through a new cultural rhetoric drawn from the worlds of business and the market place.

It is the interaction between these two forces – externally imposed and internally led change – that makes discussions of cultural change problematic. First, the two forms of change may be in direct tension. Government-imposed financial restraints often undermined internal change programmes or distorted the goals on which they were based. A classic example is the idea of 'flattening hierarchies' which, within the Tom Peters ethos, is a necessary condition for 'empowering' the front line, but which has often in reality been pursued for the rather more pragmatic reasons of reducing staff costs. Similarly 'quality' goals often became hard to pursue where services were being cut in real terms. These gaps between value led goals and pragmatic reality sometimes resulted in tensions between 'words' and 'deeds', de-motivating staff and so acting as a barrier to cultural change.

Secondly the two forces for cultural change – external and internal – may interact, sometimes reinforcing each other, but undergoing subtle transformations as they do so. 'Devolved responsibility' and 'business units' now seem to automatically go together, and both prepare the way for the externalisation of some local authority services. 'Customer centredness' seems to be a natural precursor to the market based relationships which operate both internally and externally in the local authority context. In other words, the internally led cultural change goals seem to have paved the way for, and to legitimate, aspects of the externally imposed restructuring programme.

We are now at a curious turning point. Much of the rhetoric of the 'excellence' school has become embedded in the new traditions of local authority management. But its spirit has been weakened in the face of a decade of pragmatic realism, in which for many local authorities the focus has been survival in an increasingly hostile climate, and the priorities have been managing an unending programme of externally imposed change. At the same time, a belief in the possibilities of cultural change has been tempered by experience. There have perhaps been too many examples of 'quick fix' initiatives (a mission statement here, some customer care training there) which have been superficial and unsustainable.

But at no time has the need for cultural renewal and redefinition been greater. The period of externally driven change has resulted in patterns of 'cultural impoverishment' alongside cultural change. Individual managers or sections may have been 'liberated' from many of the cultural orthodoxies of the past to pursue business goals and to meet short-term performance targets in more flexible ways. But at the same time there is a need for a unifying and coherent value base across a whole local authority, both to overcome internal fragmentation and to rebuild external legitimacy. Only if it is evident how the work of one unit or service adds value to that of another within an overall framework can a case be made for the continued existence of a local authority as a whole, based on a distinctive set of defining public service values, and informed by local choices and priorities. In the current period of national political realignment and the search for new political thinking, the renewal of the value base of local government is an important priority. While the professional and paternalistic cultures of the past have rightly been challenged, there is a need for more than the current orthodoxies of business cultures to take us into the future and to heal some of the divisions created by the recent past.

The importance of continuity

Most of the popular literature on culture (and much of the academic work) seems to suggest that the only purpose in attempting to understand an organisation's culture is in order to change it. I want to argue that it is also important to understand culture in order to draw on its past history and present richness and diversity in shaping the future. Understanding continuity – what is held to be important in the 'deep structures' of an organisation, and how that is sustained and reproduced – is vital, especially in the context of rapid change imposed from the outside. 'Managing change' can then be given a historical dimension, and change management can be understood as a process of weaving the future, drawing on, reshaping and renewing the threads of the past, intertwined with new patterns and colours. This imagery is not intended to suggest that change should be limited to that which can be encompassed as part of a continuous, evolutionary process. However, attention to cultural processes is needed in order to bring about radical changes while holding on to, or reshaping, a distinctive organisational identity.

It is an organisation's culture which acts as the most significant foundation of internal integration and synergy. Its robustness depends in large part on the ways in which change and restructurings are managed. Change which says, implicitly, that all which has gone before is worthless, or which strips an organisation of its 'cultural capital' too ruthlessly, will create permanent damage. While cultural change is often needed, this needs to be balanced by a respect for the existing culture and beliefs. It is important to recognise, articulate and celebrate a local authority's cultural strengths, grounded in local citizenship and community, accountability and equity, and to ensure that change is managed in a way which builds on these to reshape future direction and purpose.

Culture and values

As we have seen in earlier chapters, 'values' operate at the most basic and fundamental layer of culture. It is also the least manageable. It might be argued that local authorities have been through a period of 'cultural impoverishment' as old values have been eroded, and the language of 'public service' has been replaced by the new languages of business and the market-place with which many remain ill at ease. Equally, however, the unlocking of old values can be liberating. It can lead to innovation and to a refreshing period of reassessment and renewal. In the process, groups who have traditionally been excluded from decision-making can perhaps have a stronger voice.

But in moving towards 'new' values, there is a need to be clear how the tension between these and the value base of existing cultures is to be managed. Two of the value conflicts at the heart of local government change in recent years are those between efficiency and equity, and between cooperation and competition. In each, new ways of defining the agenda are required.

Efficiency and equity

The dilemma between efficiency and equity is felt sharply by both politicians and managers as they face the challenge of having to target or ration services previously available to all, or struggle to balance their commitment to being a 'good employer' and to reduce costs through moving towards a smaller and more flexible labour force. The climate of cost-consciousness and competitiveness created by recent cycles of change sits uncomfortably with other strongly held values, particularly those concerned with 'equity' of service provision.

This is especially visible in considerations of whether the greater flexibility and discretion of service managers can extend to creating different service standards for different customers, notably those able to pay for enhanced standards. Equality concerns, then, can stand in tension with the new requirements of 'customer centredness' in service delivery, although some local authorities are attempting to link equality and quality concerns by paying attention to the differential requirements of different groups of users.

Efficiency creates a further set of tensions in relation to an expanded sense of equity in terms of equal opportunity agendas for both employment policy and service provision. The demand to do things 'differently' – to change the old ways in response to equal opportunity pressures – is easily represented as a costly 'luxury' which can be foregone in the 'hard times' of limited budgets. Different approaches to, for example, staff recruitment and development or the supply of information to service users incur costs of time and other resources. When this is overlaid on greater centre–periphery differentiation, there are particular problems surrounding the maintenance of equality initiatives. Given that they have generally been developed and formulated at a corporate level, the implementation and enforcement of E.O. policies becomes more problematic with devolved or decentralised structures. Units and sub-units may allow them to fall away, viewing them as 'costs' imposed by the centre or as objectives and practices which are 'not relevant' to the particular concerns of the unit. In doing so, however, one of the core values which have traditionally distinguished public from private sector management is weakened. It remains to be seen how far the emergent language of 'managing diversity', and the recent attempts to couple business agendas with equality goals, can provide a sustainable point of renewal (Newman 1994b).

Competition and collaboration

This dilemma concerns the relationships between competition and collaboration. Approaches to managing in the new context of local government involve a whole new set of competences – how to create business plans, how to do marketing, how to carry out competitive analysis, how to write contracts and how to tender for contracts. At the same time there has been a requirement to look more towards the private sector for new models and practices. But this desperate search for the 'competitive edge' is exactly what makes some politicians feel uneasy, and which plays a significant role in persuading some able members of staff (including many women) not to take on managerial roles and identities. There is a more or less articulated sense that such competitive zeal fails to fit with the ethos, values, style of working which distinguished local government work for them in the first place. This discomfort is often difficult to express, since it is excluded by a framework which polarises the world of the public sector into choices between the old regime and the new realism and few wish to be positioned as defenders of the old regime. But what is clear is that there is a sense of loss of things valued within the old regime which appear to have no place in the new realism – collegiality, service, professionalism, fair dealing and so on.

To a limited extent, some of these concerns can be articulated with aspects of the 'new managerial' discourse of Tom Peters and others. The stress on 'honouring the front line', valuing 'people and process' and having a focus on 'quality' offers partial and unstable points of connection for 'old' values in the sense that they provide a vocabulary through which such concerns can be expressed. But precisely because the discourse is contradictory, such reference points are unstable and provoke uneasiness about 'buying into' the whole discourse by trying to appropriate some of its terms.

The dilemma between competition and collaboration is also expressed in central government policy. Although competition has been the dominant frame of reference for the restructuring of local government, there is a second and subordinate frame – that of 'partnership'. This is expressed in a variety of ways – for example, in ideas of the 'enabling authority' and in exhortations to better 'multi-agency working' – which recognise that not all public sector relations can be characterised as market or competitive ones. The logic of partnership is collaborative rather than competitive but is undercut by confusions about the intersection of the two logics (e.g., in community care there are potential contradictions between the local authority's role as enabler and purchaser – see Charlesworth, Clarke and Cochrane 1995). None the less, ideas of partnership and collaboration do address some of the experiences of, and aspirations for, public sector practice ranging from collegiality and team-working to service ideals (which are seen to transcend 'local' competitive interest).

Cultural change as a source of conflict

Chapter 2 argued that it is through culture that people make meaning of their work and develop attachments and commitments to the organisation, profession or group. Culture is also the site of conflict over meanings, and tension between different commitments and identities. These will influence, for example, the balance between different political goals within a local authority, and between the identification of members with local constituents and the local authority as a whole. They also influence how far staff loyalty will be primarily to the department or to the local authority as a whole, to the organisation or to their profession. Different identities and meaning systems will shape how far a new initiative will be viewed as unblocking old constraints, or as presenting new threats. Two of the sites of conflict over meaning and identity which are currently at the heart of local government management include those around managerial and professional identities; and between corporate and local identities.

Managerial and professional identities

Professionalism has traditionally provided one of the main sources of identity and purpose for those working in local government. Professionals have come to 'own' their field of service provision by virtue of training, peer recognition and career development, whether in environmental health or teaching. While the professional ethos has been the source of criticism about professional arrogance and paternalism, it has also been a strong institutionalised pressure for the maintenance of 'standards' and has been the basis of claims for autonomy and discretion in decision-making. Becoming a manager plays on these commitments as strong motivational factors: taking on responsibility gives power in relation to services. At the same time it requires that such commitments be balanced by a recognition of 'organisational realities' (usually budgetary ones) and by taking on board 'corporate' responsibilities. In this way, devolved management has sought to dissolve the characteristic problem of managing professionals (their split loyalties to the organisation and to the profession) not by subjecting professionals to more management but by turning them into managers. In the process, the tension between organisational and professional commitments becomes internalised rather than external. Such new managers become the focal point for conflicting identities and loyalties, struggling to reconcile in their practice the previously separated commitments. This process takes place in the context of devolved resources, which carry with them the devolution of resource limits, such that 'hard choices' are pushed down the organisation towards the front line, bringing with them the stress that accompanies trying to balance service commitments and resource limits.

Corporate and local identities

Devolved management systems also contain the seeds of a second dilemma – that of the relationship between centre and periphery or corporate and local interests. The classic bureaucratic structures of local government located control in functionally differentiated departments, each represented at the top of the organisational hierarchy by chief officers. As departments have become dissolved, fragmented or decentralised, local authorities have had to differentiate between the core 'corporate' or 'strategic' functions of the organisation and those other functions which may be effectively delegated, decentralised or contracted out. The first problem that this gives rise to is that of identifying what aspects of organisational management can be marked out as matters of corporate or strategic significance. Discussions of this issue often treat it as if the distinction was obvious and natural. However, defining the separation between 'strategic' and 'operational' issues in a local government context is complex. Any decison made anywhere in the organisation can at any moment, if it goes wrong, suddenly become of political and strategic significance.

A further difficulty is defining how to separate the centre from the periphery while avoiding the dangers of excessive autonomy for sub-units. Both aspects of this problem are the subject of organisational 'micro-politics' relating to the degree of discretion to be enjoyed by sub-units. Despite the rhetoric of 'letting go' in the new managerialism, the surrender of control by the organisational centre does not come easily. Both the powers which the centre retains and the forms of control or monitoring which they choose to exercise over the periphery can become the sites of tension, and these tensions are expressed in the form of competing success criteria within units – those of satisfying local goals, and those of meeting the requirements of the corporate centre. Performance measurement is vulnerable to disputes over what are appropriate objectives and measures, with the possibility of tensions between corporate and local definitions of desired outcomes (to say nothing of the potential difference of user perspectives).

These tensions are also expressed in the political processes of local government, in which conflicting goals and priorities are often expressed through contests around the meaning of change. What may be welcome by some as providing a new opportunity may be seen by others as undermining values which members see as basic to their political commitment. Conflicts may also surface around tensions between corporate and local priorities: for example between an economic development issue which, while being of potential benefit to the whole community, may be resisted by the local community in which the development is to take place.

The centre–periphery tension discussed above also has implications for the member role. The devolution of power to managers can be seen as a loss of control by members over issues which they wish to engage in directly, and unless a strong political role in performance monitoring and review is developed, may bring with it a weakening of political accountability. Debates about how performance is to be judged, then, must remain at the heart of the political process.

These (and other) dilemmas are an integral part of the experience of those who are both managing change and attempting to live the new cultures. As such, they link questions of individual identity and direction to the broader concerns of individual and collective survival: competitive survival; the survival of a 'public service' ethos; and individual survival in terms of continued employment. These contradictions are an integral part of the new management of local government. They will not be easily resolved by an eventual closure of the change process into a mythical future set of certainties.

Corpocrats, cowboys and cultural change

The process of renewal needs a highly motivated and committed workforce at its heart. Is is not possible to build a renewed sense of vision, purpose and direction, or to forge new styles of relationship between a local authority and its communities, on the foundation of a workforce whose own sense of purpose and commitment have been eroded. This book has emphasised throughout the importance of the human processes in the dynamics of cultural change. There are several important shifts which mean that greater attention must be paid to the 'human resources' of a local authority in order for it to achieve its goals and meet the expectations of its users and communities.

- The drive towards quality, customer focus, and responsiveness has placed a a a greater reliance on front line staff and recognition of the importance of the relationships between staff and users. Procedural and hierarchical cultures cannot do this well.

- The trend towards fragmentation, flexibility and devolution has meant that it has become harder for the centre to rely on traditional control mechanisms. New strategies of control based on contractual relationships (performance management, PRP) or affective relationships (leadership, culture, commitment) have become important.

- Labour costs have traditionally been the highest resource expenditure in public sector organisations. However as organisations 'downsize' and 'delayer', the costs of poor people management become higher. It is, then, more important than ever before to pay attention to and invest in good selection, development and other processes, and to ensure that all are engaged and committed.

- The pace and consequences of change have meant that managers have been required to develop the skills of dealing with distress, uncertainty, trauma, stress, anger, overload, loss, dislocation, and other potentially dysfunctional symptoms of complex transition processes.

The pattern of change has placed greater importance on some of the 'soft' skills in the management repertoire. For example partnerships and inter-organisational relationships require good collaborative and process skills; contract management requires excellent negotiation and communication skills. Trust has become an essential requirement of many areas of relationship, in a climate often characterised by competitiveness, defensiveness and exposure to risks. As organisations across the public and private sectors have come to deal with more complex change agendas and face more turbulent environments, many are recognising the need for new styles of leadership based on people and process skills, on enabling and empowering staff, and on involving customers and communities in decision-making – the very stuff of cultural change.

This is a long way from the mythic, heroic, and male imagery of leadership of the business literature. It is also a long way from the mechanistic and paternalistic traditions of management in local government. These two patterns correspond in part to Moss Kanter's notions of 'Cowboys' and 'Corpocrats' (Kanter 1989). Corpocrats are the corporate bureaucrats, the 'organisation men' who tend to act as trustees, be concerned with conserving resources, and who deliver dull continuity. Cowboys, in contrast, live in a world of immediate action and seek to seize every opportunity. They are heroes, champions, seeking to be the fastest gun on the street. They are insurgent entrepreneurs, and are all about dynamism, change, energy and competition.

Whether local authorities can embark on successful cultural change depends in no small part on their capacity to change their own management styles and traditions away from the mechanistic 'corpocrat' style but without moving in the direction of cowboy style business management. Many local authorities have made great progress in paying greater attention to culture, people and processes. But the 'softer' era of increased belief in participation, involvement, investment and empowerment is in many – but not all – areas being subordinated because of the perceived need to respond to new competitive environments.

Although there is still a strong element of the traditional cultures of bureaucracy and paternalism in local authorities, they have become modified as a result of organisational change. Hierarchies have flattened, skill shortages have opened up opportunitites in some areas of work, and new challenges have forced local authorities to seek out talent wherever it exists. New cultural patterns have emerged which interact with the remaining elements of traditional cultures. In many places a new form of 'macho' culture is emerging, corresponding perhaps to Moss Kanter's image of the 'cowboy' culture, which has lost many of the softening features of the older paternalistic/protective traditional culture. Internal fragmentation creates atomised units who compete with each other, and this tends to exacerbate the focus on short-term, narrow goals. Internal competition is rife; risks are high; the pressure is great; people see themselves as very exposed. It is very informal, very fast and very goal oriented, but often tends to be a blame culture.

While in many ways competition can lead to a more open culture, in which traditional divisions and hierarchies are partially eroded, it is a culture which many – including many women – find problematic. It is also a culture in which equality issues do not thrive. The challenge is to get the job done; complaints about how it gets done are seen as illegitimate. Procedures are seen as being 'in the way of' goal achievement. The shift towards competitive cultures means that women and members of black and ethnic minorities who have entrepreneurial, marketing or project management skills may be 'let in' to the club. However unless a more fundamental cultural change takes place, it remains a white and male-dominated club which will not support new ways of working (Newman 1994; Itzin and Newman 1995).

To develop a sustained process of cultural renewal something more than short-term responses to the new competitive environment is required. There is a need for a fundamental process of transformation in order to raise the performance capacity of a local authority and to change its relationships with its customers and communities over a long period. This requires the development of more open, flexible, democratic and 'empowering' orientations towards staff. It requires a greater valuing of the skills of listening, communication, networking and partnership working. It requires the creation of value adding relationships and synergies between different 'business' units and function and the development of collaborative responses to common strategic agendas. It requires a culture which actively seeks innovation and new ways of working with users and communities. It requires a more open culture which values multiple voices and draws on diverse agendas. Above all, it requires a new style of leadership which takes us beyond the 'corpocratic' style of the traditional local authority but without adopting the 'cowboy' style which can so easily surface in the shift towards leaner and more business oriented organisational forms.

Questions

In your organisation:

- *Where does a 'corpocratic' style still dominate?*
- *What are the pressures towards 'cowboy' style of management?*
- *What are the pressures towards greater attention to human processes and the creation of organisational synergies?*
- *What internal variations exist, and why?*
- *What is the overall direction of change?*
- *What does political change mean for management style?*
- *What kind of leadership is required for the future?*

CHAPTER REVIEW

This chapter has argued that:

- A process of cultural renewal is needed to counter some of the effects of previous cycles of change.
- Cultural renewal means managing the tensions between conflicting values, and balancing continuity and change.
- Local authorities must develop management approaches which support the processes of renewal as well as delivering change.

Review

From 'managing change' to 'changing management': emerging concepts and models

This book has been concerned with change. In developing the approach to understanding and managing current cycles of change it has, however, attempted to move beyond many of the traditional concerns and preoccupations of the change management literature. Much of this tends to be based on particular assumptions about the nature of change which this book has challenged. Change has tended to be seen as a series of discrete programmes and initiatives which can be implemented in a linear fashion. The assumption is that goals and strategies are pre-set and will remain stable and that the task of managers is to ensure successful implementation by persuading staff to change their ways of working. Much of the literature, then, is predominantly concerned with 'selling change' and 'overcoming resistance'.

To deal with the kinds of changes which local authorities have faced in recent years, and will continue to face, this book has argued that the tools and models of change management need to be developed and refined. First, it has been argued that there is a need to shift the focus from planning to **direction setting**. Secondly, as well as involving people in change (through participation, communication, consultation and so on) there is a need to **build the capacity** of staff to manage change effectively. Thirdly, rather than assuming that it is possible to ensure ownership of change in a context where conflicting goals and values exist, there is a need both to **build consensus** *and* to **manage conflict** effectively. Fourthly, it has been suggested that there is a need to shift the focus from introducing initiatives to that of **evaluating and learning** from those already in place. Finally, dealing with external change means responding to multiple, and often conflicting, goals. There is a need, then, to manage the tensions that these produce in order to achieve overall **organisational balance**.

MANAGING PEOPLE AND ORGANISATIONS THROUGH CHANGE

Traditional concerns	Emerging concerns
Selling change.	Managing uncertainty.
Overcoming resistance.	Managing the transition process.

Key concepts:

Planning.	Direction setting.
Participation/involvement.	Capacity building.
Communication.	Building consensus.
Ownership.	Managing conflict.
Action planning.	Learning.
Organisational development.	Organisational balance.

The book has also argued that we need to go beyond the articulation of visions and the mechanistic attempts to 'manage' culture by exploring more fully the dynamics of cultural change. Chapter 2 stressed the importance of understanding culture as subjective, as actively constructed by organisation members rather than being 'imposed' from above. Culture is the means through which people 'make meaning' and 'make sense' of their experience of work. The factors which shape the way in which this happens include:

- Language: gives us the concepts to think with and to make sense of our experience.

- Leadership: tells us how the organisation would like us to see the world; provides purpose and direction, and sometimes personal commitment.

- Symbols: send implicit or explicit signals about what is important and act as a carrier for organisational values and identity.

- Values: give us a sense of purpose and deeper meaning to our work, and provide motivation and satisfaction.

Some of the important concepts and frameworks that have been used in preceding chapters on change include:

Chapter 1   Why the challenges which local government faces require a cultural response.

Chapter 2   Culture as differentiated, contested and dynamic.

The problems and possibilities of managing culture.

Chapter 3   Cultural analysis as the starting point for change.

A layered model of culture: symbols, practices, values.

Chapter 4   Dimensions which can be used to 'map' a local authority's culture as surface change agendas.

Chapter 5   Adaptive and transformational change.

The interrelationships between structures and cultures.

Chapter 6   Shaping cultural change through changing the symbols, practices and values.

Unlocking 'vicious circles'.

Values, resistance and power.

Chapter 7   Leadership as a collective process.

Direction, consensus and conflict.

Developing leadership capacity.

Chapter 8   Learning from change.

Process evaluation.

Strategic review and strategic learning.

Chapter 9   Strategy and culture.

Organisational tensions.

Organisational balance.

Chapter 10 Cultural renewal.

Value conflicts.

Corpocrats, cowboys and cultural transformation.

There are no formulae or easy solutions. However, in developing new models, including many of those offered in this volume, the emphasis must be on seeing change as dynamic; on taking account of diversity and the politics of change; and connecting the domains of structural and cultural change, of strategy and values. Such models will enable us to move 'beyond the vision' in embedding cultural change in local government.

Bibliography

Anthony, P. (1994) *Managing Culture*, Open University Press.

Baker, E. (1980) 'Managing organisational culture', *McKinsey Quarterly*, Autumn 51–61.

Barrett, S. and McMahon, L. (1990) 'Public management in uncertainty', *Policy and Politics*, **18**, 4, October.

Bridges, W. (1991) *Managing Transition; Making the Most of Change*, Addison-Wesley.

Burns, D., Hambleton, R. and Hoggett, P. (1994) *Decentralisation: Revitalising Local Democracy*, Macmillan.

Charlesworth, J., Clarke, J. and Cochrane, A. (1995) 'Managing local mixed economies of care', *Environment and Planning*, **27**, 1419–1435.

Deal, T.E. and Kennedy, A. (1982) *Corporate Cultures: the Rites and Rituals of Corporate Life*, Addison-Wesley.

De Bono, E. (1993) *Water Logic*, Penguin Viking.

Denison, D.P. (1990) *Corporate Culture and Organisational Effectiveness*, Wiley.

Frost, P.J. et al. (eds) (1991) *Reframing Organisational Culture*, Sage.

Hampden-Turner, C. (1990) *Corporate Culture: From Vicious to Virtuous Circles*, Hutchinson.

Handy, C. (1976) *Understanding Organisations*, Penguin.

Hofstede, G. (1991) *Cultures and Organisations: Software of the Mind*, McGraw-Hill.

Itzin, C. and Newman J. (eds) (1995) *Gender, Culture and Organisational Change*, Routledge.

Kerley, R. (1994) *Managing in Local Government*, Macmillan.

Kilmann, R.H. et al. (eds) (1985) *Gaining Control of the Corporate Culture*, Jossey-Bass.

Kotter, J.P. and Heskett, J.L. (1992) *Corporate Culture and Performance*, The Free Press.

Leach, S. et al. (1993) *Challenge and Change: Characteristics of Good Management in Local Government*, Local Government Management Board.

Local Government Managment Board (1993) *Fitness for Purpose*, Local Government Management Board.

Lundberg, C.C. (1985) 'On the feasibility of cultural intervention' in Frost, P.J. et al. (eds) (1985) *Organisational Culture*, Sage.

McLean, A. and Marshall, J. (1988) *Cultures at Work*. Local Government Management Board.

Meek, V.L. (1988) 'Organisational culture: origins and weaknesses', *Organisational Studies*, **9**, 4, 453–73.

Meyerson, D. and Martin, J. (1987) 'Cultural change: an integration of three different views', *Journal of Management Studies*, **24**, 623–47.

Miles, R.E. and Snow, C.C. (1978) *Organisational Strategy, Structure and Process*, McGraw-Hill.

Mintzberg, H. (1987) 'Crafting strategy'. *Harvard Business Review*, July–August, 66–75.

Mintzberg, H. (1994) *The Rise and Fall of Strategic Planning*, Prentice-Hall.

Morgan, C. and Murgatroyd, S. (1994) *Total Quality Management in the Public Sector*, Open University Press.

Morgan, G. (1988) *Images of Organisations*, London, Sage.

Moss Kanter R. (1989) *When Giants Learn to Dance*, Allen and Unwin.

Nadler, D. and Tushman, M. (1989) 'Organisational framebending; principles for managing reorientation'. *Academy of Management Executive*, **3**, 194–202.

Newman, J. (1993) 'Women, management and change', *Local Government Policy Making*, **20**, 2, October, 38–43.

Newman, J. (1994a) 'Beyond the vision: cultural change in the public sector', *Public Money and Management*, April–June.

Newman, J. (1994b) 'The limits of management: gender and the politics of change' in Clarke, J., Cochrane, A. and McLaughlin, E. (eds) *Managing Social Policy*, Sage.

Nord, W.R. (1985) 'Can organisational culture be managed? A synthesis' in Frost, P.J. et al. (eds) (1985) *Organisational Culture*, Sage.

O'Donovan, Ita (1994) *Organisational Behaviour in Local Government*, Longman.

Ouchi, W.G. (1980) 'Markets, bureaucracies and clans', *Administrative Science Quarterly*, 25, 129–141.

Ouchi, W.G. (1981) *Theory Z: How American Business Can Meet the Japanese Challenge*, Addison-Wesley.

Pascale, R.T. and Athos, A.G. (1981) *The Art of Japanese Management*, Simon and Schuster.

Peters, T.J. and Waterman, R.H. (1982) *In Search of Excellence; Lessons from America's Best Run Companies*, Harper and Row.

Pettigrew, A., Ferlie, E. and McKee, L. (1992) *Shaping Strategic Change*, Sage.

Pettigrew, A. and Whipp, R. (1991) *Managing Change for Competitive Success*, Blackwell.

Quinn, R.E. (1988) *Beyond Rational Management: Mastering the Paradoxes and Competing Demands of High Performance*, San Francisco, Jossey-Bass.

Ranson, S. and Stewart, J. (1994) *Management for the Public Domain: Enabling the Learning Society*, Macmillan.

Sackmann, S.A. (1991) *Cultural Knowledge in Organisations; Exploring the Collective Mind*, Sage.

Schein, E.H. (1984) 'Coming to a new understanding of organisational culture' in Salaman, G. (ed.) (1992) *Human Resource Strategies*, Open University Press.

Schein, E.H. (1985) *Organisational Culture and Leadership*, Jossey-Bass.

Stewart, J. and Clarke, M. (1992) *The Learning Local Authority*, Local Government Management Board.

Stewart, J. (1995) *Understanding the Management of Local Government* (2nd edn.), Pitman Publishing.

Storey, J. and Sissons, K. (1993) *Managing Human Resources and Industrial Relations*, Open University Press.

Williams, A., Dobson, P. and Walters, M. (1989) *Changing Culture: New Organisational Approaches*, Institute of Personnel Management.

Index

Index

McLean, A. 15, 96
McMahon, L. 107, 109, 110
management approach 10–11
management changes 5
management development 92
management practices 29
management relationships 4
management skills 158–9
management style 122, 123
managerial culture 52–3, 156
mapping
    cultural dimensions 59–62
    strategic tensions 138–9
Marshall, J. 15, 96
Meek, V.L. 22
members 31, 122
Miles, R.E. 45, 46
Mintzberg, H. 68
missions 90, 100
models 89–90, 101–2
monitoring 129, 136
moralist culture 51
Moss Kanter, R. 159
motivation 112–15
motivators 89

new beginnings 111–12
Nord, W.R. 21

observation 34–5
O'Donovan, Ita 42–3
officers 31, 122
one stop shops 2, 134
open approaches to change 71
open culture 52
operational issues 157
organic approaches 95
organisational balance 132, 162
    diagnostic questionnaire 139–46
organisational changes 5
organisational culture *see* culture
Ouchi, W.G. 9, 45, 46

172

outcomes, evaluation 125
outsiders 20, 36, 93

partnership 1, 3–4, 155
Pascale, R.T. 9
peers 89
performance management 122
performance measures 32
person culture 47, 48
Peters, Tom 9, 15, 151, 155
planning processes 122
policy narratives 100
political processes 12, 157
political relationships 4
post hoc learning 122
power 19, 89, 92–3, 96
    two-way flow 57
power culture 46, 48
practices 26, 82
    changing 86–7, 96
    diagnostic questions 30–2
pragmatist culture 51
precipitating pressures 69
proactive culture 58–9
process evaluation 125–6
process oriented culture 49, 50
processual learning 122–3
producer driven culture 54–5
professional culture 52–3, 156
progress 112–13
public interaction 31
public service values 26
publicity materials 28
purchaser/provider framework 9–10
purpose 113

quality 1, 5–6, 151, 158
    case study 87–8
    definitions 19

radicalism 70, 72–3
Ranson, S. 8, 19